A Country in the Mind ↝

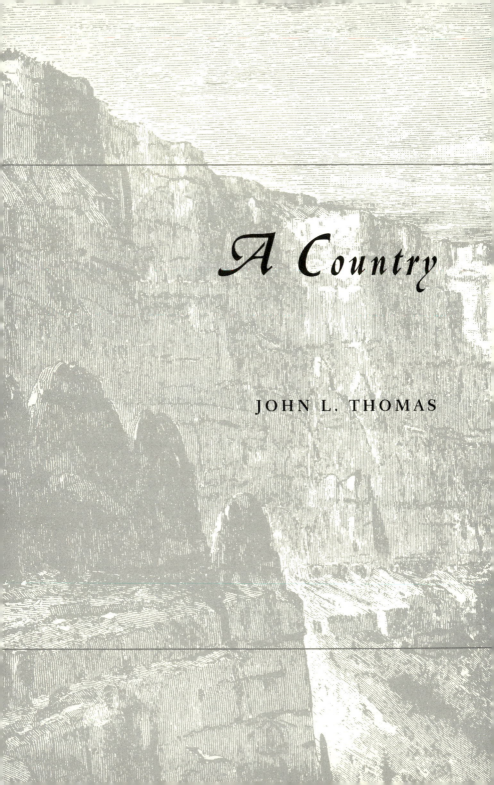

A Country

JOHN L. THOMAS

in the **Mind**

Wallace Stegner, Bernard DeVoto,

History, *and the* American Land

ROUTLEDGE

New York / London

A volume in the series Culture/Society/Politics, edited by David Nasaw.

Published in 2000 by
Routledge
29 West 35th Street
New York, New York 10001

Published in Great Britain by
Routledge
11 New Fetter Lane
London EC4P 4EE

Routledge is an imprint of the Taylor & Francis Group.

Library of Congress Cataloging-in-Publication Data

Thomas, John L.
    A country in the mind: Wallace Stegner, Bernard DeVoto, history, and the
American land / John L. Thomas.
       p. cm.
    Includes bibliographical references and index.
    ISBN 0–415–92781–1
      1. DeVoto, Bernard Augustine, 1897–1955—Criticism and interpretation.
2. Literature and history—West (U.S.)—History—20th century. 3. Stegner, Wallace
Earle, 1909—Criticism and interpretation. 4. DeVoto, Bernard Augustine,
1897–1955—Friends and associates. 5. Stegner, Wallace Earle, 1909—Friends and
associates. 6. American fiction—20th century—History and criticism. 7. American
fiction—West (U.S.)—History and criticism. 8. Conservation of natural resources in
literature. 9. Wilderness areas in literature. 10. West (U.S.)—Historiography.
11. West (U.S.)—In literature. 12. Landscape in literature. 13. Land use in literature.
14. Commons—West (U.S.) I. Title.

PS3507.E867 Z94 2000
813'.52093278--dc21

                                                    00–036631

Title page: An alcove in the Red Wall. (From *The Exploration of the Colorado River and Its Canyons*, J. W. Powell, 1895.)

For Blake and Chandler

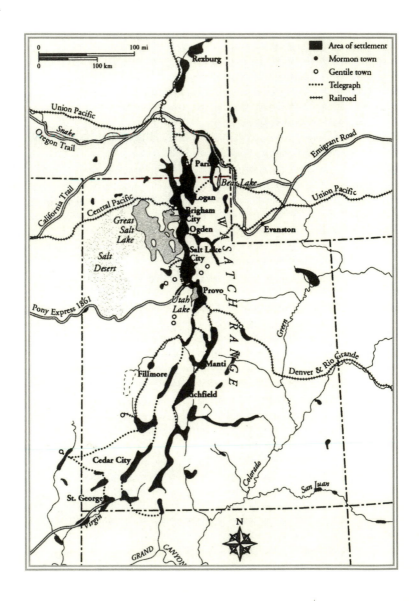

Mormonland, 1890.

Contents

Prologue

Overleaf: Kanab Canyon, in the Red Wall Limestone. (From *The Exploration of the Colorado River and Its Canyons*, J. W. Powell, 1895.)

I have spent a good part of my intellectual life tracking what I have called "Alternative America" across time and space from antebellum communitarian experiments in New England and the Burnt-Over District of New York to post–Civil War theorists and reformers in Illinois coal mines and California wheatfields and on to twentieth-century plans for migrations out of metropolises into a producerist countryside. The phrase itself is elastic, not to say elusive, bending and fitting itself to varying developmental winds blowing across the country over the years. Whatever political concessions the idea of an Alternative America has been forced to make to voters and politicians, the vision of another way—a middle road between a profit-driven market economy on the one side and a repressive collectivism on the other—has enjoyed a long if not always happy life.

In the years before the Civil War the advocates of a cooperative alternative to Jacksonian scrambles for spoils opted out of the rat race, as they thought it, and formed a number of voluntary communities as a means of educating their fellow citizens and converting them to a better life. Not many of these experiments survived competition with an aggressive entrepreneurial capitalism, and those that did were apt to have been gathered Christian communities—Shaker, Mormon, Oneidan—willing to forgo material wealth for spiritual health. The more secular communities, like that at Roxbury's Brook Farm or those at nearby Fruitlands and Hopedale, collapsed under the weight of constitutional baggage piled on by members struggling to find the exact balance between collective need and individual freedom. Yet taken together even in their failure, these communitarian experiments signified a profound unease with rampant developmental capitalism and a conviction that individual aspirations and social energies could be peacefully harmonized by the simple application of social mathematics.

Despite the shortcomings of their social analysis and their various utopian arrangements, the communitarians left an ethical legacy for post–Civil War reformers equally disgusted with the rapacity of Gilded Age businessmen and their political pals. The principal spokesmen for an Alternative America in the later years of the nineteenth century were the reform theorists-turned-activists Henry George, Edward Bellamy, and Henry Demarest Lloyd. George's balanced utopia was the creation of a single tax, his magic device for preventing the monopolizing of land and ensuring the stability of the nation's small communities. Bellamy envisioned a cooperative mass society organized as an ethical army practicing a religion of solidarity by employing the techniques of mass production and distribution to provide complete equality. Lloyd in his turn offered a vision of an Americanized Fabian socialism that would harness the power of the federal government to secure a decent life for all Americans. It is worth noting that all three men were writers and journalists critical of Gilded Age excess who became vigorous reformers and turned to politics as a means of realizing their ethical vision. Aspects of the thought of all three men appeared in Populism as it emerged out of the Farmers' Alliance in the early 1890s, in particular its call for the assertion of national authority in behalf of beleaguered little people working the land.

Just as the late nineteenth-century reformers borrowed some of their ethical precepts from their antebellum predecessors, so they themselves left a legacy of their own to twentieth-century recipients. Among them: Upton Sinclair with his moderate socialism and End Poverty in California campaign; Benton MacKaye with his communally constructed Appalachian Trail; Lewis Mumford with his call for a fourth migration out of the American metropolis into the countryside. These and a whole host of independent intellectuals in the first half of the twentieth century helped themselves to fragments of the adversarial tradition which they pieced together, adapted, and modified to suit their various purposes. Common to all their efforts was a vision of a democratic participatory ethic as the source of a renewed civic spirit. Here in barest outline is an alternative tradition undergoing all kinds of permutations over two centuries but retaining throughout the vision of a civic entity situated in a middle ground between capitalist consolidation and control and coercive collective management.

Now there appear two other recruits to the ideal of a national commons owned and cared for by all the citizenry—Bernard DeVoto and his friend Wallace Stegner. At once artists and reformers, novelists and historians, they shared a recognition of the increasingly dire need to save wilderness, protect parks and forests, and prevent further degradation of the West, which was proceeding rapidly with the consolidation of corporate capitalism. Both men railed against the spoilers and their apologists, and called for an expanded role for the federal government even as they criticized the shortcomings and inefficiencies of its bureaus and agencies. Friends, occasional colleagues, warm admirers of each other's work, they offered a vision of citizen stewardship over the American land with directives coming from Washington and implementation supplied by enlightened local citizens adhering to a shared land ethic. In other words, an environmental alternative to the wastage and spoliation practiced by corporate giants.

I launched my exploration of DeVoto's and Stegner's Mountain West from the other end of the country—from Somes Sound, which splits Maine's Mount Desert Island nearly in half. Vest-pocket-size Somes Sound is the only fjord on the eastern coast of the United States—"It is a small fjord, sir, but there are those who love it." Only a slice of the sound's eastern and western shorelines belongs to Acadia National Park. The rest is private land dotted with massive gray-shingled "cottages" of the old elite mingling now with outsized trophy summer homes of the new rich. Looking down the sound—or better still, paddling down it in my battered Old Town canoe—introduces me to a tiny checkerboard national park, a magnificent juxtaposition of deep woods, glacier-made lakes and ponds, manageable mountains, and storied rockbound coast, all tossed together in limited acreage. Paddling the sound or hiking the park's numerous trails and carriage roads, I experience a sensation not unlike the one I get strolling the national Mall in Washington—a keen sense of personal but also joint possession. This park belongs to me, I found myself thinking, to me and all the rest of the American people jointly. I soon became an advocate of parks, preservation, and wilderness.

With these sentiments I began my imagined journey to the Mountain West, and Bernard DeVoto and Wallace Stegner became my guides. Although I knew them both as novelists, essayists, and literary critics, it was the history they wrote that introduced them—DeVoto's magnificent trilogy of the discovery, settling, and exploitation of the West, and Stegner's moving account of his beloved hero, John Wesley Powell, visionary planner for the country west of the 100th meridian. It was their history which reminded me of the half-life of Alternative America living on as a call for environmental wholeness in an age of rampant consumerism.

Subsequently I read much but not all of their work, ignoring for the most part DeVoto's fiction, which struck me as not up to the standard of his history, and selecting from Stegner's huge output those novels and stories that threw light on his environmental ideas. Nor have I probed DeVoto's or Stegner's private lives. In explaining his intentions in undertaking the biography of his friend, Wallace Stegner said that some things in DeVoto's life were "nobody's damn business" and that "the way his head worked and what he did with his head" were what mattered. So here. In this set of matching portraits, their ideas and what they did with them are my concerns. A sympathetic critic of an early draft of these profiles urged me strongly to "get out of their heads." My rejoinder, had I thought of it, should have been, "But that is where the action is."

All this by way of explanation if not apology. Both men have been well served by biographers, DeVoto by Stegner's masterful account of his difficult life, and Stegner himself by Jackson Benson's perceptive study of a long literary career. So I have indulged myself in a couple of the liberties accorded the portraitist: foreshortening, arbitrary selectivity, and ample quotation. This book, then, is an account of a necessarily distanced but intense intellectual friendship based ultimately, as Stegner said, on *liking* someone. I hope this work makes clear that I like both men and consider them intellectual friends.

Legacy

Overleaf: Kanab Canyon, near the junction. (From *The Exploration of the Colorado River and Its Canyons*, J. W. Powell, 1895.)

I ⤳

In the March 1951 issue of *Harper's* Bernard DeVoto, the irascible, pugnacious, and seemingly inexhaustible editor of "The Easy Chair" feature, boldly faced down his newest enemies, the "humble sheep-walker" and the "bronzed horseman" riding out of the fabled West and into Washington bent on another raid on the public lands. In a hard-hitting article entitled "Two-Gun Desmond Is Back," DeVoto watched their legislative approach warily and warned his readers to beware of yet another landgrab by organized grazing interests, this time under the guise of a cut in fees. Four years earlier he had helped fight off an even bolder move to repeal the Taylor Grazing Act and return all public land in the West to the several states. Now the same predators were back again "bellyaching about bureaucratic tyranny" and bent on "taking back" what they mistakenly considered their land. Their fraudulent claim was the product of a major miscalculation, DeVoto announced in appealing to public opinion. "You have got to know about it because it is your property they want to alienate." The national forests, he reminded his readers, belong to the American people, and by far their most vital function in the West is the preservation and protection of watersheds in an otherwise arid land. "Vital parts of every important watershed in the West are in the national forests—and stock-grazing is a threat to a watershed the moment it becomes overgrazed." It was just this kind of destruction by benighted special interests that the larger American public would have to prevent. "You had better watch this, now and from now on," DeVoto admonished his readers. "The land-grabbers are on the loose again and they can be stopped only as they were before, by an effective marshaling of public opinion." The people's property was at stake, their money was subsidizing a raid on their own wealth. "You had better make sure that your Representatives and Senators understand clearly what is going on and where you stand. Then if you don't belong to one of the conservation societies, join one and keep in touch." Americans would need to be on their guard, keep their eyes open, and continue to "walk the bounds" of their collective commons.

When he sounded his warning in 1951 DeVoto had been walking the bounds of his native West for three decades, accompanied for nearly two of them by his friend, colleague, and eventual biographer, the Western writer Wallace Stegner whose steadying companionship he cherished and whose recent recruitment to environmentalism paralleled his own. Together the two friends constituted a model of the engaged intellectual, DeVoto confronting predatory grazing, mining, and timber interests in his native region and drafting environmental statements for Adlai Stevenson's 1952 presidential campaign, and Stegner continuing to rally the nation's growing environmental forces for four decades. Both men were sons of the Mountain West. DeVoto was born in Ogden, Utah; Stegner, twelve years younger, arrived in Salt Lake City as an adolescent in the early twenties and came to call the Arid Region home.

By the time they met in the late thirties, Stegner had already published his University of Iowa doctoral dissertation on Clarence Edward Dutton, the geologist colleague of John Wesley Powell, and was also the author of a novel, a prize-winning novella, and some half-dozen short stories and essays. The two met in Chicago at a convention of the Modern Language Association after Stegner had written the older man thanking him for his part in awarding the Little, Brown Prize for Short Fiction to his *Remembering Laughter*. They met again the following summer—1938—at the Bread Loaf Writers Conference in Vermont when Stegner was asked to join the fiction writers' group. Soon he was making final corrections on his third novel, assembling notes for a fourth, and collecting memories that would take shape in his compelling auto-biographical novel, *The Big Rock Candy Mountain*. For his part, DeVoto, by the time he turned west for research and revitalization in 1940, had written three novels about his home country and another on Boston in the year of the execution of Sacco and Vanzetti; dozens of short stories under the pen name John August; as many hard-hitting articles and reviews for the *Saturday Review of Literature* and *Harper's*; plus a bruising defense of his favorite author, Mark Twain, against the attacks of the literary "coterie" of Eastern intellectuals. To call Stegner and DeVoto compulsive achievers is to understate the case and underestimate both men, who over the next fifteen years would use their talents to help form and direct a growing environmental movement. Their examples of conversion and continuing contribution serve as guideposts in a later and more threatening phase of the struggle over the American environment.

II ↳

Bernard Augustine DeVoto was born at the foot of the Wasatch Mountains on January 11, 1897, the son of an apostate Catholic father and a lapsed Mormon mother whose joint defections may have supplied their offspring with a lasting example. More certainly, they gave him affection and support—intellectual stimulation and grudging approval from a contrary-minded father, adoration from a doting mother who, DeVoto remembered, "lived to be very proud of me," for having a son at Harvard "symbolized dizzy grandeurs to her." Her death in the influenza epidemic of 1919 plunged her wildly ambitious but deeply insecure son into a two-year, paralyzing depression from which he finally extricated himself by writing his first novel. From his father, Florian DeVoto, "the finest mind I've ever known" but also the most difficult personality an adolescent could confront, he inherited a hair-trigger temper, a censorious outlook on the world, wild impatience, and an undying hatred of sham. Mathematical genius, mineralogist, assayer and abstracter of titles, and according to his son, a "complete misanthrope," Florian held it "dishonorable for one to make money where he [had] scorned to do so." Though generous and fundamentally kind, he was a determined failure, convinced that the world was composed of fools and liars. But he was also, his son recalled with lingering admiration, "a gentleman of the old school, ferociously upright, reactionary, a lover of the classics . . . an unreconstructed states rights Democrat who hated Bryan but voted for him, who despised Roosevelt and who belongs exactly and completely to that simpler day when there were men and principles in politics." Throughout his own lifelong excursion into the world of American history DeVoto would arrive at many of his father's ethical judgments while at the same time freeing himself from Florian's paralyzing cynicism.

The adolescent DeVoto cast himself heroically in the role of the lone outsider, intellectual superior, and scoffer at the pieties and certainties of a Mormon establishment. He looked the part of a feisty intellectual—short, slightly pudgy, a moon face framed by glasses and with a nose squashed against his face by an errant baseball. The young man carried his defiance of the world with a swagger which became a lifetime posture. Wallace Stegner pieced him together from a collection of contradictions: "precocious, alert, intelligent, brash, challenging, irreverent, literary, self-conscious, insecure, often ostentatiously crude, sometimes insufferable." The verdict of a sister of a schoolboy friend was more succinct and withering: "The ugliest, most disagreeable boy you ever saw." The boasting and bragging would become muted in maturity but not the adversarial temperament nurtured by a profound insecurity. Wallace Stegner, who also suffered moments of shattering self-doubt, traced his friend's "incomparable knack of infuriating people" to a nagging lack of confidence that blunted his social sense "of how much was enough":

how far to go in colloquialism among those who spoke only the stiffest king's English, how far to go in profanity among those whose mouths had early been sterilized with soap, how far to go in familiarity with reserved strangers or friendly women, when to stop tomahawking the body his intelligence and eloquence had slain, how much to resent an apparent slight, how not to turn simple disagreement into insult, how to state his opinions, which were quick, powerful, and sure, without stating them at someone's expense.

Social graces all, Stegner admitted ruefully, which his friend and mentor never managed to acquire.

DeVoto's career was set inside an intensely felt personal history of a postfrontier upbringing "in between" the mountains and the metropolis, midway between wilderness canyons above and industrial wasteland below, both within distance of a bicycle ride from home on the edge of the foothills and encroaching sagebrush. Young DeVoto's third-generation Ogden was a world in which the frontier survived, in his telling phrase, as "fossilized memory," its mountain men, cowboys, rustlers, and train robbers enshrined in myths of derring-do. The mature historian, driven by a lasting boyhood urge to set the record straight, would spend an entire career correcting these and other regional fictions and attacking the booster state of mind which nourished Mormon society. In explaining his obsession with facts and lifelong irritation with the purveyors of fictions, he once wrote, "You see, it's the concrete thing, the living thing, that I go for, and the abstraction from it repels me."

Many of those concrete facts lay buried in his boyhood waiting for memory to excavate them. An essay written for *Harper's* in 1935 uncovers DeVoto's ambivalent attitude toward his home country and its history, skillfully mixing reminiscence with cultural conclusion. In "Fossil Remnants of the Frontier" (April 1935) he announces himself, as he had done for fifteen years, as the dry-eyed demolitions expert armed with the facts and determined to blow sky-high every fable, figment, or fabrication of the Western past he encounters. *The American Indian of legend?* "I have not found him a beauty lover, the creator of a deeply spiritual religion or an accomplished metaphysician who plumbs eternal secrets which his brutish conqueror could never understand." Call it racism and philistinism, if you must, DeVoto warns the "best minds" of the Eastern intellectual establishment, but "sybilline women and rapt men from megalopolis have been unable to persuade me that neolithic culture was anything but neolithic culture." *What about frontier violence of storybook fame?* The era of violence in the Mountain West ended in "a forced equilibrium" imposed by the Mormon Church on the city of Ogden and the whole state of Utah, and "very little strife found its way to the children." The cost of that peace, however, has been steep, not to say prohibitive. The Church of Jesus Christ of Latter-Day Saints built "a semi-cooperative society governed by an oligarchy who claimed divine sanction and exercised absolute power." The chief influence of Mormonism on his own postfrontier generation, DeVoto scoffed, was "to spice it with miracle. In few societies are angels as common as policemen and heaven rather more familiar than a city park." *And culture in Ogden's brave new world?* Mormonism has long pronounced its blessing on a commercialized consumerism bequeathed it by an industrial East. "Luncheon clubs arrived, and Chautauqua, the Y.M.C.A., the syndicated press, booster movements, the hysterias and compulsions of wartime and prohibition, and the liberal point of view and national prosperity." It was no wonder, then, that a bright, intellectually ambitious young man had escaped as soon as he could.

Yet at this point in his recollections of his Ogden boyhood he paused—as he would in everything he ever wrote—to introduce a contradiction that enormously complicated the process of making judgments and confounded the would-be critic. Ogden in a postfrontier age, oddly enough, was home to an "all-inclusive freedom that touched every aspect of our lives." The liberating force came as wind off the nearby mountains. "By the time we were eight we went on daylong explorations of the foothills, miles from home, unsupervised by older people. Two or three years later we were beginning to climb the peaks, and by the time we were fourteen we were camping out for days at a time, without tents, in the canyons up the range." The several canyons running east up into the Wasatch Mountains offered a temporary escape from the pieties and rigidities of Mormon society, and the young DeVoto frequently availed himself of hiking paths and trout streams in upland country that was still open but within easy reach of civilization below. Weber Canyon, the largest, winding south out of

Ogden had served as an entryway into the valley for Mormon settlers and California-bound wagon trains. In DeVoto's childhood and youth it furnished the pass through the mountains for the railroad which ran past his grandfather's farm, where the boy spent part of his summers. "Almost wilderness," Wallace Stegner called it in likening the country to the canyons winding out of his own hometown Salt Lake City across "middle ground" and up into the peaks. Though no athlete, the adolescent DeVoto was a tireless hiker and already the crack shot that would make him a stateside Army instructor during the First World War.

This brief holiday DeVoto recalled as the principal frontier remnant—an interval between two ages. A fragile frontier system had collapsed within memory, but the new industrial order had yet to lay its deadening hand on Western life. The original frontier had disciplined children by necessity; the rising industrial system taught its children, albeit haphazardly and inconsistently, a new ethic of humanitarian responsibility. "Our order granted them the frontier freedom and then, omitting discipline, disregarded them. In some ways it was not a bad system."

Ogden in the early years of the century was a grimy industrial city of some forty thousand which straggled up from railroad yards and smelters in the bottomland through the business district and past palatial Mormon homes like that of the Mariner Eccles family and on up to lower-middle-class duplexes on the margins of respectability where the adolescent DeVoto grew up. By his own admission he was not well adjusted to an environment of Mormon prosperity and piety. "These people are not my people," he explained to a friend on his return to Ogden after his years at Harvard. "Their God is not mine. We respect, hate, and distrust each other, and though self-defense forces me to take them with much humor, nothing forces them so to take me." He never changed his mind.

Ogden's social system, in all events, was sufficiently open to allow a budding intellectual the freedom to try on various identities as intellectual tough, cultural snob, literary aspirant, and—more realistically—ambitious poor boy. The homes of wealthy and pious Mormons remained closed to the interloper, and young DeVoto earned his pocket money for tobacco and books by working on the interurban line between Ogden and Salt Lake and serving a brief stint as a stringer reporting for the Ogden *Evening Standard*.

As an older DeVoto looked back on his own postfrontier upbringing he realized that he had been a "laboratory specimen," the unknowing recipient of an endless variety of influences and forces shaping his idiosyncratic view of the world, connections and relationships that escaped all attempts at categorizing. One of his grandfathers had been an early industrial mechanic from England drawn to Utah by Mormon missionary zeal into a life of hardscrabble farming. His other grandfather was a onetime Italian cavalry officer turned commission agent. "I played with sons and grandsons of Hawaiian princes, Scandinavian murderers, German geologists with dueling scars, French gamblers, Virginian slave owners, Yankee metaphysicians," he boasted with pardonable exaggeration, "of men who came from everywhere, who had every conceivable tradition, education, and canon of taste and behavior." There was, in short, none of the deadly uniformity imputed to Western life by Eastern "best minds." "I grew up in a culture more various than I have found anywhere else."

DeVoto began his search for the Mountain West's true past as an adolescent, collecting bits and pieces of regional lore and family history in hopes of discovering a meaning that would satisfy. Affronted as he was all his professional life by the interpretive intrusion of Eastern observers bent on teaching him the significance of his legacy, DeVoto early on countered with his region's acceptance of a Darwinian truth that no wishful thinking of liberals and would-be reformers could alter. "To that people [of the Mountain West] the struggle for existence is not something that can be repealed by Act of Congress or demolished by rainmakers, philosophers, or community meetings in prayer." Here announced with authority and not a little arrogance, was DeVoto's version of *insiders history* based on close personal scrutiny of a province of meaning closed to outsiders. Ogden—indeed the entire state of Utah—he could see only after leaving it in the early twenties, had been the "damndest place." "We were really fin de siecle, we were the frontier's afterglow. We saw that glow fade out, we stood, as it were, on a divide, and also went down the other side."

The image of the watershed—the great divide between epochs and stages of development—was more than a metaphorical adornment for DeVoto. The chain of mountains stretching up the continent from New Mexico to Montana, Idaho, Washington, and beyond, dominated as towering geological fact the cities and their inhabitants in the valleys and plains below. In between lay the middle ground of his childhood years—uplands, rising layers of benches and empty desert leading up gulches and canyons from stands of alder, aspens, and cottonwoods near water to groves of oak, walnut, and fruit trees along the high line planted there by determined farmers like DeVoto's Mormon grandfather, Samuel Dye, who briefly made the wilderness bloom.

The foothill ridges above Ogden also marked a temporal divide for the fledgling historian—a sundering of stages of development into three discrete segments which could be identified and classified as frontier, postfrontier, and industrial. From this vantage point in the center of the middle ground a whole epoch unfolded—for DeVoto, Willa Cather, Walter Prescott Webb, Wallace Stegner and a whole host of chroniclers of the Arid Region and the Mountain West—the meaning of which he read as declension from the short-lived achievements of the pioneer generation to the civic disintegration and spiritual barrenness of the industrial age. Insofar as the aspiring writer out of Ogden admitted to possessing a philosophy it rested on the observed signs of decline combined with the challenge of renewal.

DeVoto's education was a migratory one, as though the young provincial already sensed that the cultural wind blew from the East however much he disliked the huffing and puffing of its intellectual purveyors. In 1914 at the urging of a motherly teacher "who lived for literature," he enrolled in the nearby University of Utah just in time to witness a battle over academic freedom. In the spring of 1915 two young English instructors, one of them DeVoto's teacher, were fired, presumably at the behest of a disgruntled Mormon Church, whereupon fifteen faculty members resigned in protest, the American Association of University Professors investigated and blacklisted the institution, and the president ultimately resigned. By this time DeVoto was long gone, having been accepted by Harvard and having scraped up the money to attend. At Harvard the study of history interested the would-be writer from Ogden less than courses in literature and composition offered by the genial Barrett Wendell who, DeVoto recalled, taught American literature "as a now abandoned folkway of the Bostonians," and by the more imaginative Charles T. "Copey" Copeland and Dean LeBaron Russell Briggs. One of the pieces of personal luggage the ambitious writer carried from Ogden to Cambridge was a strong provincial pride which sat oddly beside his curt dismissal of Mormon money-grubbing. Arriving on the Harvard scene as an outlander, moreover, provided a greater range for self-advertisement, this time as the rough-and-ready

Westerner, tough-minded and no-nonsense, coarse-grained but the genuine article. Ogden may have been the cultural wasteland he pronounced it, but it was also the gateway into the mountains and the shards of memory waiting to be assembled into an intensely personal history.

When the United States entered the First World War, DeVoto abandoned his truculent antiwar stance and enlisted in the Harvard Regiment in April 1917, serving for the duration as a stateside instructor in markmanship. At Fort Devens he found time to ponder a novel he had been considering for some time. "And what a book it is!" he rhapsodized to his parents. "It is the novel of my own country, the wide and ample theater of the hills, the peaks and valleys, the mountain streams, the railroad, above all the people. *Labor amoris.*"

In 1919 he returned to Ogden to nurse his mother through her final illness, a wrenching experience that tipped him into a deepening depression that marked his last year at Harvard. By 1920 he was back home again, despondent, "confronted by the terrible truth that I am doing nothing, but am wasting my time while life slips away—and the more terrible truth," he confessed to a friend melodramatically, "that my ability and even my desire are diminishing." Sunk in "self-abomination and despair," he painfully recovered his emotional balance by writing an occasional piece for the *Standard*, teaching American history to local junior high school students, a task to which he warmed, and exploring the surrounding canyons as he plotted his first novel, which appeared in 1924 as *The Crooked Mile*.

The Crooked Mile, like its immediate fictional successors, *The Chariot of Fire* (1926) and *The House of Sun-Goes-Down* (1928), drew heavily on local, family, and regional history, sources DeVoto would mine with much greater skill in his nonfiction. For it must be said that though an extraordinarily talented historian, DeVoto was not a particularly compelling novelist. All of the qualities that made his history so authoritative—a constant personal presence, strong opinions, commanding interpretive voice, ironic distance from his actors, and a highly stylized language—combined to make his fictional characters speak aphorisms, his plots to meander, and the experience of reading his novels strenuous and, in the end, wearying. "He never persuaded you about his people," Wallace Stegner observed. "He wanted to judge, he wanted to denounce, he wanted to express his own ideas and his own feelings. He wasn't willing to suppress himself quite enough—or didn't know how." Such is the case with *The Crooked Mile*, a piece of juvenilia which traces the decline of the frontier from the energetic founders and builders of the first generation to the pillagers and spoilers of the third. But the novel is also the tale of the conversion of a world-weary young man suspiciously like the author himself from cynicism to belief, hopeless detachment to direct engagement with the land. The agent of young Gordon Abbey's salvation is the mordant historian Jonathan Gale, another authorial alter ego, who provides his ward with an understanding of the meaning of the frontier and the will to put it to use in reclaiming his inheritance.

This first novel is a thematic prologue to DeVoto's major historical work: the making and unmaking of the frontier through three generations. The protagonist Gordon Abbey's grandfather, Jim Abbey, left the defeated Confederacy for a new freedom cultivating the unpromising land in the foothills above Windsor (Ogden), turning desert into gardens and orchards and refusing the main chances that might have made him rich. Instead, Jim Abbey pinned his hopes on extending the frontier beyond the mountains and building up the country. In this visionary project he lost his shirt and died a failure. His son and Gordon's father, Pemberton Abbey, now dead, was a failed Veblenian engineer, the inventor of the Abbey Process for refining copper, who had been bilked by corporate predators. Thus Gordon Abbey in the third generation inherits little in the way of a patrimony or a usable past until he returns to the remnant of his grandfather's upland orchard, brings it back to life, and carries on the old man's scheme for securing a second chance across the mountains.

Despite his limitations in plotting action and drawing convincing characters, DeVoto's descriptive power and his use of symbolic landscape were impressive. Here are the dark satanic mills of Windsor-Ogden standing at the center of the twentieth-century purgatory:

> Down where the Ophir and Windsor rivers joined, the copper mills and the Dunlap factory had spread out over the land where cottonwood stumps were still standing. Steel frames grew into long sheds and were filled with machines. Floodlamps played on them by night, and in some of them a green leprous light illuminated a second shift. . . . Sixteen hours in the twenty-four the machines rocked, the men labored before them and fires of three colors poured intermittently from the portholes. . . . At intervals guards carrying shotguns stood in the shadows atop the stockades. A wheel that seemed half the wall of one building revolved with a methodical, herculean force. A jet of yellow fire at the porthole became a geyser of flame, picked out walls and tracks for a mile around and receded into nonentity. There was a shrill hum, almost too high to be heard; it was felt, rather, a vibratory chorus of countless belts and chains, discs, teeth, stamps, movable arms, conveyors, rollers. . . . Westward the Ophir river had

shrunk to a trickle between cottonwoods. Eastward the night sky ended against a line of heat-parched peaks.

DeVoto's nightmare world is crowned by the mountains, source of copper for the syndicate but also emblems of the primitive freedom of wilderness. Gordon Abbey and a friend explore their lower reaches:

They plunged into a narrow gulch that led downward between vertical gray walls where not even juniper could lodge, along dry courses of spring freshets that had heaped stones and boulders among dead limbs. The long twilight of the canyons deepened moment by moment. . . . Dusk was deep in the gulch and a flare of purple sky with sunset at its mouth, when they came to a spring splashing up through the dead leaves where a cedar grew against the cliff. Three-fold darkness from the gulch, the tree, and the sunken sun.

In between mountain fastness and industrial wasteland lies, ready for recovery, the abandoned middle ground of Jim Abbey's upland farm and the pasture where he dug his first irrigation ditch sixty years earlier. Returning to reclaim his inheritance, Gordon Abbey surveys the ruins now his to repair:

Sweet clover and burdock waistdeep choked the path to the front door, and a grass snake slid away into the thicker growth at Gordon's approach. The doors were unhinged, the windows frameless, the walls torn and scratched. One chimney had fallen in, but the floors and beams were sound after fifty years and the roof would turn rain. . . . The barns and sheds, what remained of them, were in ruins. . . . But the two orchards near the house and the flat place that had been given to the kitchen gardens and the pasture were unkempt. The orchards, in spite of the weeds that choked them, raised boughs heavy with blossoms.

Unlike his fictional creation who stays on to reclaim his ancestor's land, in 1922 the twenty-five-year-old author escaped the confines of home with an instructorship in English at Northwestern, but with the firm intention of returning to Cambridge and Harvard as soon as he could. As Wallace Stegner pointed out, DeVoto's first novel was part of the twenties literary canon of the revolt against the village, his protagonist "a sibling of Claude Wheeler, Carol Kennicott and George Willard" and, perhaps, "a somewhat remoter kinsman of Jake Barnes." In decamping the provincial premises DeVoto fired two parting shots, one at his hometown and the other at the entire state of Utah. Two essays—"Ogden: The Underwriters of Salvation," published in a 1925 collection entitled *The Taming of the Frontier,* and "Utah," which appeared fittingly in the March 1926 issue of H.L. Mencken's *American Mercury*—targeted Mormons and Gentiles alike in denouncing the provincial smugness and pretensions of the effete descendants of rugged pioneers who had once "shouted maleness from the Peaks." The renegade's judgments of Senator Reed Smoot's Utah domain were even harsher. Here Mormons lived lives of unquestioning obedience to benighted elders. Gentiles, for their part, contented themselves with retailing "a farrago of lies about polygamy." Business leaders limited their reading to the bottom lines of their developmental deals, and serious thought throughout the state languished. "Civilized life," DeVoto explains to an incredulous Cambridge matron, "does not exist in Utah. It has never existed there. It will never exist there."

The outraged response of Utah readers to these "postfrontier correctives," as their author styled them, was predictable: Florian DeVoto reported from Ogden a flood of telephone calls warning his son never to show his face there again. Years later DeVoto would disavow both pieces as "ignorant, brash, prejudiced, malicious, and what is worst of all, irresponsible," the work of a "young buck, intoxicated with the newly achieved privilege of publication." But he had been considered a "sissy" and a "pansy" in Ogden, "widely snooted and derided" for publicly declaring his intention to write. "I resented it violently. . . . In some degree [the articles] were acts of vindication, in some degree acts of revenge." Their immediate effect, however, was to "raise the historian's conscience" in the brash cultural critic who in the aftermath of their publication defended both articles as calls for "the free play of intelligence" and "the interplay of ideas" on the ground of history.

DeVoto taught in the English department at Northwestern from 1922 to 1927, lecturing irreverently, reading student themes with a sharp critical eye, and marrying one of his students, Helen Avis MacVicar, who in the coming years would frequently prove as outspoken as her husband. Avis, one of DeVoto's Harvard students recalled, was "the only faculty wife who might have said 'horseshit' even to President Lowell." DeVoto joined the English faculty at Harvard as a lecturer in the fall of 1927, teaching writing part time while working overtime as editor, essayist, novelist, short-story writer, and all-round professional polemicist. In 1936, denied promotion to permanent status, he quit and accepted the editorship of *The Saturday Review of Literature*. Within a few years there he acquired a well-earned reputation as a skilled adversary and a dangerous intellectual enemy, always forthright to the point of pugnacity, occasionally wrongheaded, but almost always in full command of his cherished "facts," and equipped, moreover, with a

Bernard DeVoto, according to his friend Wallace Stegner, was a divided self. Shown in a publicity photo taken in the 1940s is the public combatant, the fearless defender of the American land and the fastest gun in the East ready and willing to face down every would-be despoiler of the West. (COURTESY OF THE DEPARTMENT OF SPECIAL COLLECTIONS, STANFORD UNIVERSITY LIBRARIES.)

consuming love of controversy. DeVoto was a bad man to cross but easy to love if, like Wallace Stegner, you were inclined to agree with most of his pronouncements.

Over the years, DeVoto found that his spiritual home lay increasingly with the historians—in Cambridge, Paul Buck, Arthur Schlesinger, Sr. and Jr., Crane Brinton, Samuel Eliot Morison; in New York, Columbia historians Henry Steele Commager and DeVoto's former Northwestern colleague Garrett Mattingly. To his professional confidant Mattingly he admitted that "half of my old dichotomy is a historian, not a critic. . . . In history you know what

Here in this 1950 photograph at the summer Radcliffe Publishing Procedures class is the "other self" noted by Stegner—the sensitive and sympathetic listener preparing to offer advice and support. (COURTESY OF DEPARTMENT OF SPECIAL COLLECTIONS, STANFORD UNIVERSITY LIBRARIES.)

you're talking about—or . . . at least you partly know." Though he frequently felt unloved by his academic competitors or, worse, dismissed "as a phony, charlatan, and menace to the public peace," he began to contemplate a three-part study of the frontier a decade before the first volume *The Year of Decision: 1846* saw the light. "I see history as primarily processes of individuals," he told Commager after the first volume appeared, and he declined an invitation to contribute a study of the Jacksonian frontier for Commager's *The Rise of the American Nation* series because he said he lacked "the vast statistical acquaintance with people, places, racial stocks, frontiers and counties and settlements, crops and finances and elections, congressional debates, and all the paraphernalia." This latter disclaimer rang hollow, for already by the mid-thirties, he was acquiring a prodigious knowledge of the details of western expansion. Steadily across the decade he widened his original focus to include national politics and developmental policies haphazardly fashioned in the East and misapplied throughout the trans-Mississippi West. Yet his entry into this larger national history was through the familiar territory of the Mountain West he knew so well. A decade after publishing his first novel and ten years before the appearance of *The Year of Decision: 1846* he straddled the line between fiction and fact in an essay for *Harper's*, "Jonathan Dyer, Frontiersman" (September 1933).

The *Harper's* essay drew on family history: changing the first name and adding a terminal "r" to the Dye name to mask his identity, DeVoto told the story of his maternal grandfather, one of the West's little men through whose uncomprehending life could be traced an entire social process. The thinly veiled biographical sketch opens in the year 1852 with a young Hertfordshire mechanic's conversion to Mormonism by American missionaries, his subsequent firing, and his decision to leave for the New World. "We are concerned with Jonathan Dyer," DeVoto warns, "not because he was persecuted for his faith but because that faith merged him with the strongest current in the New World from which the missionaries came." The new convert settles briefly in Boston, moves to Brooklyn, and then heads west for Deseret and a farm backed up against the Wasatch Mountains and the Weber River. Here with a loan from the Church, Jonathan Dyer launches his one-man assault on the desert. His grandfather, DeVoto hastens to add, was a man of no ideas whatever: he willingly acquiesced in his lowly place inside a hierarchical society, followed orders from above, and uncomplainingly set to work making the waste places bloom. It was never a matter of what Jonathan thought, for ideas did not drive his world. The waves of resentment and revolt that swept across Utah in the last half of the nineteenth century washed over him without leaving a trace.

Here DeVoto pauses in his account of his grandfather to summarize the larger meaning of his life of quiet acceptance and determination. "Revolutions are always struggles between social groups; only propaganda tries to make them seem the will of the people in action." Throughout time the majority of people, like Jonathan Dyer, are largely unmoved by grand notions and stirring pronouncements. They neither consciously will nor purposefully act but instead patiently endure, "and in the end pay tribute to the old group victorious, or to the new one which has cast it out." Farmers, in particular, give their lives to their land and generally remain voiceless. Jonathan Dyer, like agrarians across the centuries, is "a mere name invoked by speculators who are their self-consecrated champions. They have paid taxes, gone bankrupt for the profit of adventurers, and served as the stuff of financial and political exploitation. From Rome to the valley of Easton [Utah] there has been no change."

Such sweeping dismissals of the possibility of controlled change and intended reform were the fruits of DeVoto's reading in the early 1930s—together with Harvard faculty including L.J. Henderson, Talcott Parsons, Elton Mayo, Joseph Schumpeter, and DeVoto's friend Crane Brinton—of Vilfredo Pareto's *Trattato di Sociologia Generale*, "the hardest-boiled book I have ever read," he confessed in explaining how the Italian engineer-sociologist was changing his thinking about politics and society. Pareto denied that ideology accurately represented inchoate reality. Instead, all societies rest on "residues," nonrational clusters of customs, habits, and attitudes which give rise to "derivations," those rationalizations and justifications that constitute the sentiments on which people rightly or wrongly act. Ideas, DeVoto readily agreed after wading through Pareto's lengthy analysis, were in fact simply convenient rationalizations comforting in their indistinctness for those unknowing actors walking the stages of history. So, at least, it seemed to him as he tried to make sense of his grandfather's life on the frontier. Neither an activist nor even much of a thinker, Jonathan Dyer found meaning in hard work and limited wants until he was able to move from dugout squalor to medium-magnificent frame house, escaping destitution for a hard-won competence. Sagebrush furnished the index to the scanty entries in the journals in which Jonathan kept his accounts. "Jonathan hacked at that hellish growth. Spines and slivers that no gloves can turn fill one's hands, the stench under the desert sun is dreadful, and the roots, which have probed wide and deep for moisture, must be chopped and grubbed and dragged out inch by inch." Together with his neighbors working in forced cooperation, Jonathan digs the canals and ditches that bring water from the mountains, and gradually extends his acreage, borrowing from an exacting Church and in turn selling his produce to its members high and low. When the railroad comes through, he hauls timber for ties and breaks rocks for the grades. Goods begin to arrive at the farm—store-bought shoes, stoves, books and the candles to read them by.

Political ideas and public events continue to pass Jonathan Dyer by—the Morrisite War ignited by a false prophet and fought next door to his farm, the suppression of polygamy in which he had never believed, ongoing skirmishes with Utah's Gentiles. Neither philosophy nor theology impinged on his life. He was, his grandson tells us, only "a unit in the process that made and remade the nation," his homestead a tiny nucleus in a sour land he was laboring to make sweet. Mormonism was the perfect instrument for reclaiming this unpromising land. It rewarded the faithful and frugal, supplied him with needed rules, and told him to vote Republican so as to advance Israel and his own prospects in tandem.

What, finally, can be made of the life of Jonathan Dyer? Singularly little, says his grandson, save for a single all-important fact: "A fruit grower by divination," he made the desert flourish.

There was here—nothing whatever. A stinking drouth, coyotes and rattlesnakes and owls, the movement of violet and silver and olive-dun in white light—a dead land. But now there was a painted frame house under shade trees, fields leached of alkali, the blue flowers of alfalfa, flowing water, grain, gardens, orchards. . . . This in what it had been a dead land. . . . There had been nothing at all, and here were peaches, and he had come eight thousand miles. That is the point of the frontier.

But the frontier quickly passes, Jonathan grows old, and after his wife dies, he leaves the farm for town. His place is sold, his orchards cut down, and a speculative fox farm appears in its place. Senile in his last days, he wanders the roads trying to find his way back home. He dies in 1923. But the fox farm collapses with the twenties boom, and a few years later Jonathan's grandson receives a letter with the news: "They are farming your grandfather's land again." Perhaps, DeVoto muses, there will again be orchards and kitchen gardens, but if not, the fact of Jonathan Dyer's life still stands: "He came from Hertford to the Great American Desert and made it fertile. That is achievement."

DeVoto carried to Cambridge all of the values he celebrated in the life of his grandfather. His estimates of New England were various but generally favorable. New England's metropolis was Boston with Cambridge and Harvard as its intellectual core, its hinterland Vermont's and New Hampshire's hill country, where he spent as many summers as he could manage. In the rural back-country of the region he found the same producerist outlook and steadied view of the world he had admired in his grandfather Dye. In rural New England, however, republican producer values survived in an older culture which had passed its prime and now nurtured habit rather than reflection. This storied New England had been grievously misunderstood by smart-aleck intellectuals, and DeVoto immediately on arrival demanded a correction. Always in need of adversaries and antagonists to keep himself in fighting trim, he settled in and instantly took up cudgels against the "guild" of public intellectuals and cultural critics, many of them New Yorkers, who had so misread New England and its people. Intellectuals, he sneered, prided themselves on holding the "right ideas," one of which was the condescending notion that New England was repressed, overcivilized, decadent. He had to admit that the Sacco-Vanzetti tragedy seemingly gave at least partial credence to their judgment: he himself had served on a committee that had vainly tried to save the anarchist pair from Brahmin vengeance. Nevertheless, the nation's history demonstrated that New England was not alone in making mistakes, and he still considered it better equipped by its past to soften class conflict than any other region of the country.

But it was the rocky upland farms and pastures and the huddled villages stretching across Vermont, New Hampshire, and Maine that struck the outlander from the West as the real New England. Here was Robert Frost territory where self-reliant folks left you alone and minded their own business. This New England wore its late Calvinist heritage with defiance; its citizens rejected ideas of perfection out of hand and seemed to agree with their observer that the best that could be hoped for in a flawed world was a hard-earned "resolution of imponderable forces" that permitted relative social stability and communal harmony. Yankee proof, in short, of Pareto's hypothesis. This meager but honest reward was one that New England had won for itself by dropping out of the national race for power and wealth, and in so doing "was delivered from a great deal of noise and stench and common obscenity" and rewarded with a measure of "relief, decency, and ease." New England's country road had branched off the main American highway to Illimitable Progress and ended instead in a reasoned adjustment to reality allowing it to cope with the Great Depression when the mills shut down and four-percents plummeted. As for their own slim rations out in the countryside, New Englanders had "had hard times for sixty years—in one way or another for three hundred years." They had been forced to find a way to endure "perpetual depression" and had found it.

In his visit to his Vermont friend Jason, a saturnine jack-of-all-trades, DeVoto traveled to the edge of sentimentality if not caricature—to Titus Mood country ("Hi, Bub!") where Vermonters who are the genuine article all say "a-a-a-yuh" on the intake to save breath while agreeing tartly that indeed life is a "hahd" case. At a deeper level, however, new friend Jason in Depression Vermont and grandfather Dye in late nineteenth-century Utah are kinsmen—populist producers with limited expectations but an unerring sense of reality which tells them that in the end the piper must be paid. The two men, each in his own time, were consummate realists: "accidental by-products" of a harsh nature and grudging history, which combine to make Utah a retrievable haven and the Yankee commonwealth "the almost perfect state."

These rural fastnesses along the northern New England tier, DeVoto admitted, made up only part of the region and were wholly unlike the decaying industrial cities—Lowell, Lawrence, Lynn, Pawtucket, Woonsocket—that scarred the landscape with their "ulcerous growths." "To spend a day in Fall River," he agreed, "is to realize how limited were the imaginations of the poets who have described hell." Still, noxious as they were, such cities were slated to disappear. The outlander from the Arid Regions found something appealing and almost familiar in the empty canyons of Depression New England mill towns—long deserted streets and alleys running between huge rocklike mills, windswept empty lots with crumpled newspapers plastered against their wire fences like tumbleweed. And as for the decrepit seaports—Newburyport, Salem, Portsmouth—"they are marshes now." Lawrence and Lowell would soon slide into the Merrimack, and Salem return to wetlands: "The unpolluted sea air will blow over them, and the Yankee nature will reclaim its own."

All this reclamation DeVoto believed possible because as America's first frontier, New England was now a "finished place." It had achieved that stage of equilibrium which his reading of Pareto convinced him was the best social state that could be hoped for in an imperfect world. In scale and lingering civic spirit New England followed the examples of Florence or Venice while the rest of the nation went chasing Rome and empire. In Frederick Jackson Turner's scheme of moving frontiers New England stood as the first completed section. "It is the first old civilization, the first permanent civilization in America." It was also as close to utopia as a chronic unbeliever would ever get, and, as he was gradually coming to understand, even contemplating it would involve abandoning Pareto for direct political engagement.

No such New England sunset awaited the West, DeVoto realized, a region still caught in the throes of colonization by Eastern business interests—banks and mortgage companies, promoters and developers, financial operators and corporate giants. Following Walter Prescott Webb through the arid West, with Webb's *The*

Great Plains in hand, DeVoto promptly agreed that beyond the 100th meridian the traditional American frontier culture had simply broken down. Meanwhile farmers and settlers waited for the arrival of the industrial tools they so desperately needed—gang plows, harrowers, harvesters, fencing, windmills and artesian wells—machinery which sank them deeper and deeper in debt. Here was the cause of a permanent state of Western dependency, the fate of a debtor section but with a difference. The West's abundance, DeVoto reminded his "Easy Chair" readers in 1934, had been there for the taking all along, but instead of being recycled through the regional economy it had been siphoned off by greedy Eastern manipulators and despoilers in the form of corporate profits. As the Great Depression descended on the entire West, DeVoto's initial hopes for recovery fell with it. The twentieth-century Westerner seemed to him the innocent victim of an empire-building financial colonialism run out of Wall Street and aided and abetted by the "governmental stupidity" of Washington. "Looted, betrayed, sold out, the Westerner is a man whose history has been just a series of large-scale jokes."

But then came the New Deal, which at first DeVoto watched apprehensively but with mounting, if still grudging, appreciation as the thirties wore on. By the time he issued his gloomy report, the recovery of Western land and water was already under way, engineered by the Bureau of Reclamation and steered by the firm hand of the Department of Interior's crusty Harold Ickes. Ickes's word to the West was "dams," more and more of them as the thirties progressed: Boulder Dam, as it was called in the New Deal years, the multipurpose giant built at a cost of $114 million and more than fifty workers' lives, creating Lake Mead, which extended 115 miles up the Colorado. Parker Dam, below Boulder, sending electric power across the Four Corners in all directions. The Colorado–Big Thompson Project, authorized in 1937 and completed in the fifties. Fort Peck Dam on the Missouri, a monster construction bringing irrigation as well as electricity to the arid Great Plains. And hard by DeVoto's hometown the Pine View Dam in Ogden Canyon, funded by Ickes's PWA and irrigating some seventeen thousand acres of nearby farmland.

Land management under New Deal auspices proved a more contentious business with stockmen and grazing interests resisting enforcement of the Taylor Grazing Act of 1934, designed "to stop injury to the public grazing lands by preventing overgrazing and deterioration, to provide for orderly use, improvement, and development, to stabilize the livestock industry dependent upon the public range." Implementing these bold promises was another matter as enforcement of the Taylor Act immediately encountered the thorns and thistles of local resistance and business opposition. There followed throughout the thirties and across the Second World War verbal range skirmishes at home in the West and political forays against Washington, both of which DeVoto watched with a censorious eye until by 1947 he was able to add benighted stockmen to his growing list of enemies.

When, in 1936, DeVoto was denied tenure in Harvard's English department, he moved (temporarily, as it turned out) to New York City to attempt to breathe new life into the venerable *Saturday Review of Literature* and, more successfully, to fill *Harper's* "Easy Chair." With his appearance at both magazines the decibel level of New York's political and cultural debates reached a new high. As editor and contributor DeVoto fought a war on two fronts against equally talented and contentious adversaries. On the left stood communists, socialists, and fellow travelers of all sorts but also left-wing independents like Edmund Wilson. On the right the cultural prophets Lewis Mumford and Van Wyck Brooks held forth and continued to receive a patented DeVoto pummeling. Asked by a nettled Edmund Wilson to declare his own principles for a change, DeVoto jumped at the chance. First and last, he replied, he objected to "gospels." "I early acquired a notion that all gospels were false and all my experience since has confirmed it. . . . I distrust absolutes. Rather, I long ago passed from distrust of them to opposition. And with them let me include prophecy, simplification, generalization, abstract logic, and especially the habit of mind which consults theory first and experience only afterward." Here were the principles announced as prejudices on which he was already building his history of the American West.

DeVoto's eccentric liberalism was fed by an abiding fear of collectivism and coercion in any form but also by a nagging personal itch to set Easterners straight on Western ways and people. Beneath his battle of words with various New York intellectuals lay a genuine if measured appreciation of the New Deal and President Roosevelt for whom he voted steadily if usually with some skepticism. He could agree, as he later told his friend Elmer Davis, with "perhaps forty percent" of the New Deal's thinking, "and about sixty percent of its ad hoc measures." He distrusted FDR's attempts to strengthen the executive branch at the expense of Congress and the Court, but he welcomed virtually all of the New Deal's regional development and reconstruction initiatives, especially those bringing environmental relief to a hard-pressed West with soil erosion controls, forest reserves, dam building, county agricultural agents, and Forest Service proposals.

In May 1940 DeVoto, accompanied by his young historian friend Arthur Schlesinger, Jr., headed west to visit his home country for the first time in fifteen years. They followed the old Santa Fe Trail down which would soon march many of the heroes in his history of the fateful year 1846. Then northward through deserts and Jackson Hole to Ogden where he was joined by his wife, Avis, and their older son, Gordon, (the baby, Mark, having been left in Cambridge in the care of a trained nurse). Then eastward once more through Montana and the upper Midwest to the Great Lakes, the St. Lawrence, Québec, and back to New England.

Out of this prolonged excursion came four "Easy Chair" pieces and an article entitled "Main Street Twenty Years After" which curiously reversed his indictments of six years earlier. Westerners, he discovered, had regained their equilibrium along with their financial stability. Prohibition was gone and with it that pinched anxious scowl of housewives who now joined their husbands for a beer in the local bar. Schools were improved. Roads were better and so were the roadside amenities dispensed by new motels and gas stations. Green lawns in drive-through Midwestern towns. Busy stores and markets. Clearly he had underestimated the resilience of the Western temper and the political will in Washington. "The economic system in the years of its collapse," he admitted, "has somehow contrived to distribute goods more variously and more deeply than it ever did in the years of its vigor." And the environment from the Mississippi to the Great Valley appeared marvelously improved as well. Shelter belts, irrigation ditches, roadside parks, fish ponds and hatcheries, firebreaks and lookout towers. "It is the more heartening," he concluded after admitting that much remained to be done, "to see the progress that has been made against the forces of disintegration, forests growing in logged-out areas, dams holding water in midsummer that started downstream in a flood in April, and land being built where land had been allowed to blow away." Small beginnings, perhaps, but "a palliative of our daily despair" as Americans finally realized the desperate plight of Europe's democracies. DeVoto's own war with the Eastern intellectuals flared off and on for the rest of his life, but as world war came to the United States in 1941 his quickened sense of national power and pride, muting a sour populist particularism, seemed to promise a new dispensation for his home region and a renewal of a national environmental will.

III ⌐

Wallace Stegner did not share DeVoto's impressions of Harvard and Cambridge or his estimate of New England's redemptive example. Both men as writers and teachers successively worked their way east, DeVoto from Evanston's Northwestern in 1927, and Stegner twelve years later after graduate work at Iowa, a frustrating semester teaching at fundamentalist Lutheran Augustana College in Rock Island, Illinois, and an instructorship at the University of Wisconsin. Both men arrived at Harvard to find themselves on the fringes of the university's academic community. DeVoto taught vigorously until denied tenure, but Stegner voluntarily picked up stakes after five years, choosing to settle in Palo Alto for "a lifetime of writing about the country I had grown up in." He later confessed that "teaching at Harvard, which should have gratified my highest ambition, didn't fully satisfy because I didn't much like the place where Harvard was situated. I took the first opportunity that offered a chance to get back west." When Stanford dangled a professorship in creative writing before him, "I came like a nine-inch trout on a copper trolling line."

New England's rural backcountry, on the other hand, retained its strong appeal to Stegner and his wife, Mary, as it did for the DeVotos. In quitting Harvard for the West, Stegner was forced to abandon temporarily an ancient Vermont farmhouse which he and Mary had bought and repaired before coming to Cambridge and to which they returned for several summers until gas rationing during World War II put an end to their vacation sojourns for a while. By 1947 when he published *Second Growth*, a loosely knit string of vignettes of village life along the northern New England tier, he could claim to know that insular world "reasonably well" since in many ways it reminded him of his childhood. He also agreed with his fellow Bread Loaf Conference veteran Bernard DeVoto that upcountry New England was a finished civilization. "This is a static society," announces one of his characters, an interloper like the author himself from academia, "a dying village in a dying state. In spite of everything wonderful in it, laboriousness, traditions as binding as laws, the whole state's a backwater. It's a little tribal backwater, a survival, and it doesn't lead anywhere." History had touched its yeoman families once during the Revolution and moved on, leaving behind village greens rimmed by low-slung colonial farmhouses and upland pastures, leading back to the hills with their "abandoned houses and barns the color of tarnished silver" collapsing quietly as "little by little the spruce marched in from the woods and engulfed the meadows, took them back."

All his life Stegner confessed to a profound attachment to place and considered it a limitation on his imaginative powers yet at the same time the source of all the creativity he possessed. "I have an exaggerated sense of place," he told an interviewer in the 1980s as he reviewed his massive literary output. "I also have a feeling that my personal experiences are all I surely know, and those experiences are very likely to be rooted in places." In Cambridge, though befriended by the DeVotos, he admitted to being homesick for the red rock country of the plateaus and the clear air of eight thousand feet. It was here in the West's high country that place and the historical imagination converged in his mind. As a freshman at the

University of Utah he had been assigned geologist Clarence Dutton's *The Geology of the High Plains of Utah* (1880) and found himself "by pure accident" in Dutton's pages right in the middle of the high plateau of southern Utah where his family had a cottage. On Fishlake Plateau, "all of a sudden history crossed my trail" as he discovered on his hikes "what had happened there sixty, seventy years before" and traversed ground that would become sites for six national parks and monuments in his lifetime. In Cambridge he missed Bryce and Zion, Grand Canyon and Capitol Reef and the Granddaddy Lakes wilderness. "I had left the whole West, and I began to realize how lucky I had been to see so much of it. I was also beginning to realize how deeply it had been involved in my making."

Wallace Stegner, like Bernard DeVoto, was a child of the Mountain West, but his route to Salt Lake City, where he spent his adolescence and early manhood, was a wildly circuitous one. Twelve years younger than his friend, Stegner was born in 1909 on his maternal grandfather's farm in Lake Mills, Iowa, and in the first ten years of his life experienced a succession of uprootings. His father, George, who would appear in thinly fictionalized form as the harsh, domineering father in several of Stegner's best short stories and as the brutal Bo Mason in his autobiographical novel, *The Big Rock Candy Mountain*, was the exact opposite of DeVoto's grandfather Samuel Dye. George was a drifter, plunger, and born loser with "a wicked temper," overbearing manner, and a foolish faith in the main chance who chased his perpetually receding goal across the entire West, from a North Dakota wheat farm to a logging camp in Washington's Cascades to a scruffy little town across the international line in southernmost Saskatchewan to a succession of stops in Salt Lake City, Hollywood, and Reno. "My father was a boomer," Stegner explained as he looked back at his childhood from an emotional distance of nearly three-quarters of a century—a gambler, bootlegger, rainbow chaser, as "footloose as a tumbleweed in a windstorm." Which made young Wallace a true son of the West, "born on wheels" and "shaped by motion," yet coming to rest in two crucially defining places—the postfrontier town-in-the-making of Eastend along Saskatchewan's Frenchman's River at the foot of the Cypress Hills during World War I and in that odd mixture of piety and promotionalism that was Salt Lake City in the twenties.

Compensating, perhaps, for the forced mobility of his early years, Stegner retained indelible memories of images and sounds but also smells which later recalled the precise place for him and attached meaning to it. The single spot of sun on a tent in the dark forests of Washington's logging country. The buttery smell of breadcrusts dispensed from a dishpan in a Seattle orphanage where his mother was forced to leave him and an older brother for a while. Or standing in an Eastend garden with a Chinese laundryman and truck gardener laughing under a hot sun with a ripe tomato in his hand. The fledgling novelist Bernard DeVoto compacted his memories of times and places and then scattered them lavishly throughout his narratives. Stegner's recollections found form in evocative short stories, memoirs, and vignettes that suggest rather than dramatize and leave the reader with a sense of life once lived but of meaning discovered only in the act of writing.

The key to this process of discovery for Stegner the child observer and the reflective mature writer alike was *history* as the single source of identity—the means of locating oneself in the flow of time from past to present. History in this intensely personal sense he later described as the building of a pontoon bridge across one's life, an ongoing work of construction that stretched from a remembered past on one shore toward an unknown future awaiting on the other. Looking back at his childhood years from the distance of old age, he could see that as a boy he had "yearned for continuity" as the only way of finding out who he was and where he belonged. Was he American or Canadian or by ancestry Norwegian? Was he a son of the prairies or a townsman in the making? A life of successive uprootings and temporary replantings exacerbated the child's sense of dislocation and discontinuity, convictions that could only be checked by the permanence, real or imagined, of place and the paths made across it. The history he studied in school seemed impossibly distant from his life—"somewhere off both in time and space, off at the edges" of his mind. "I don't know what I thought reality was," he confessed later, "but it wasn't anything you read about." Instead, it was what you remembered.

Stegner's sharpest memories centered on the six childhood years in Eastend, Saskatchewan, and the surrounding prairies. "The shaping years of my life," he called them, adding, "I have never forgotten a detail of them." Hardly an exaggeration. Sometimes memory needed jogging by recovered sights and sounds, but just as often it was a smell, as it was on his return to the town of his boyhood forty years later in search of "an ancient unbearable recognition" in an odor "pungent and pervasive" which at first he could not place yet knew instinctively had "always meant my childhood." Crossing the little bridge to town over the muddy stream, he sniffs the river water and the mud along the banks, then the railings of the bridge and the wild rose and dogwood growing along the path. "Nothing doing."

And yet all around me is that odor I have not smelled since I was eleven, but have never forgotten—have dreamed, more than once. Then I pull myself up the banks by a gray-leafed bush and I have it. The tantalizing and ambiguous and wholly native smell is no more than the shrub we called wolf-willow, now blooming with small yellow flowers. It is wolf-willow, and not the town or anyone in it, that brings me home.

A child's point of view, Stegner once observed, is peculiarly limited; he sees what is in front of him and only later comes to connect what he has experienced with a larger world of meaning "and so comes to make perception serve inference." The writer later recalls riding out to the prairie homestead as a little boy in his father's battered touring car and sitting there "alien and noticeable"—an augury of failure to come in his father's doomed attempt to grow wheat where nature refused to cooperate.

I remember that high-square car, with its yellow spoke wheels and brass bracing rods from windshield to mudguards and its four-eared radiator cap. It stuck up black and foreign, a wanderer from another planet. . . . We sat baldly on the plain, something the earth refused to swallow, right in the middle of everything and with the prairie as empty as nightmare clear to the crawl and shimmer where hot earth met the hot sky. I saw the sun flash off the brass, a heliograph winking off a message into space, calling attention to us, saying "Look, look!"

Or the April day in town in 1917 when Pop Martin's dam gave way and the bridge went out, presaging the collapse of the developer's real estate enterprise.

One of the rails snapped free and hummed out over the tormented web of wood and steel, and the air was crystallized with its gong-sound. We felt it in the roots of our teeth. In one ponderous rotating motion the bridge bowed and went down, and the backed-up ice and water pushed over it and buried it in a wash of yellow foam, spit it up again and floated it, poles and ties and braces in a bound-together tangle, and wrenched it loose from its roots and washed it away down river.

The "nontown" of Eastend, as Stegner remembered it, was just a step removed from the hell-on-wheels of a Canadian Pacific construction camp, consisting chiefly of a raucous boardinghouse for the crew building a branch line down from the railhead town of Swift Current sixty miles to the northeast. The Stegner family— hot-tempered, bullying George and his long-suffering wife, Hilda, elder son, Cecil, and Wallace, an undersize "mama's boy" and object of his father's scorn—spent their first winter in Eastend in an abandoned railway dining car, and the next in a rented shack before George built a four-gabled house and barn down by the river. Eastend with its initial 117 inhabitants sat on the doorstep of the Cypress Hills up Chimney Coulee, a miniaturized version of DeVoto's Ogden beneath the Wasatch range. The town's history dated from the day-before-yesterday in the late 1860s when the Hudson Bay Company turned its territory over to the Mounties, who built a post in the hills which the Blackfeet promptly wiped out. A few years later cattlemen with their herds drifted over the line from Montana, and from their ranch house at the Z-X spread dominated the town until the blizzard of 1906–1907 put them permanently out of business. On the remains of that disaster George Stegner and his neighbors built their town. They built it haphazardly and with no awareness of history and the constraints it imposed on entrepreneurial energies. Like boosters and boomers in any age George Stegner and his fellow townsmen sought to escape history through an act of will and an urge to seek the main chance. If history taught lessons in limits, forget it!

Nature, however, was scarcely kinder to the Stegner family than it had been to the cattlemen. What young Wallace could not realize at the time but later with the help of Frederick Jackson Turner came to understand was that he, like DeVoto a few years earlier, had grown up as a witness to the closing of the frontier—"the very last demoralized end when it was quite impossible way out in the dry country—when the homesteading and small farm, free land frontier came to a kind of dribbling end, not with a bang but a whimper."

Yet Stegner remembered Eastend as a good town for a boy to grow up in. Behind the frame house his father built stood a cut-bank and a wooden bridge over the muddy stream where there was swimming in the summer and skating throughout the long winters. There were picnics, as well, and hunting excursions out on the prairies and up into the Cypress Hills. Also chores—pasturing his broken-legged colt on a nearby empty lot, toting buckets of water from the river, hacking off the rock-hard frozen hindquarter hanging in the winter shed. In all of these scenes the figure of George Stegner loomed ominously, a constant menace whose rage knew no bounds and who could explode at any moment, a tormentor given to abject contrition, which the boy found worse than the punishment. George Stegner was determined to bully his frail and frightened son into submission, all the while demanding that he be a man. There was the time when Wallace, six years old, was caught playing with his father's loaded .30-.30 hanging over the mantel and received a savage whipping, after which the youngster lay behind the chopping block watching his "big dark heavy father" working, and "all the time I lay there I kept aiming an empty cartridge case at him and dreaming murder." Usually he could count on his gentle mother's intercession, but not on one occasion when "he clouted me with a chunk of wood and knocked me over the woodbox and broke my collarbone." Stegner carried into manhood a mixture of hatred, pity, and contempt for his father, finally propitiating rather than forgiving him in a later autobiographical novel, *Recapitulation* (1979).

Guns played a large part in Stegner's boyhood as they did in DeVoto's. He admitted to having been a sickly runt "but hardly a tame one." Like all his companions he was given a gun and from the age of nine or ten used it with pent-up ferocity. "We shot at everything that moved: we killed everything not domesticated or protected," trapping, shooting, snaring, and poisoning every furbearer they could find. "Nobody could have been more brainlessly and immorally destructive," he confessed, even though "there was love too" and the knowledge acquired from studying his kills. "I lived contentedly at the center of my primitive culture soaked in its folklore, committed to its harsh code of conduct even when I despaired of living up to it." For like his gentle mother, he was a "nester" at heart, saddened to leave his father's failed homestead for the forbidding world of Great Falls, Montana. "I loved the place I was losing, the place that years of our lives had worn smooth."

Reflecting on his formative years in Eastend, Stegner recovered a younger self cut off from community and deprived of history. "I was a kind of lone particle, and I was looking for something to attach to." Books, instead of expanding and enlarging the unformed intelligence, fragmented and dispersed it. The little formal history available to him described distant monuments and legendary sites, suggested faraway museums and relics resting on marble, "emblems of a storied past." "We knew no such history," the author recalled, "no such past, no such tradition, no such ghosts." Eastend's vernacular museum was the dump ground, the collecting point of the town's trash and the memories attached to it, at once "the kitchen midden of all the civilization we knew" and the town's "first communal enterprise." Eastend's primary institution attached its families to the day-before-yesterday with rusty barbed wire, baby carriage wheels, melted glass and lead casings, an abandoned office safe and all the relics with which the town memorialized its recent past. The dump also recorded the more personal history of its inhabitants. The skeleton of a colt, badly crippled and still wearing iron braces on its forelegs, had belonged to young Wallace who succumbed to paternal advice to turn him over to a foreman of a nearby ranch where presumably he could be better cared for. "A few days later I found his skinned body with the braces still on his crippled legs, lying on the dump." Books littered the dump ground, among them a set of Shakespeare that George Stegner had carried from North Dakota to the West Coast to Eastend only to lend them to a neighbor's daughter who discarded rather than returned them, a lesson in the prodigality and wastage involved in making a new country. "We had so few books that I knew them all; finding those thrown away was like finding my own name on a gravestone."

This private history registered on the town dump supplied a crucial sense of self-definition for the maturing writer who readily confessed, "I may not know who I am, but I know where I am from," meaning "a dung-heeled sagebrush town on the disappearing edge of nowhere." Real history, in young Stegner's personal experience, was a different realm from the domain of the academicians and professionals. It filled an inner need by supplying the odds and ends out of which the older man could build a meaningful world, a task which became more and more urgent with advancing age. "I don't suppose that I missed history," Stegner admitted, "until I was at least middle-aged, and then I realized that I didn't have a single place to which I could refer myself." He had never really had a crowd or a gang, no core or particular context "except as I could find it or form it by going back along my life." The journey toward self-understanding involved leaving the dump ground with its collected clues to the past and crossing over to a middle ground lying between remembered fact and invented fiction, a terrain Stegner would traverse frequently in the course of a long career. "I think to become aware of your life, to examine your life in the best Socratic way, is to become aware of history and how little history is written, formed, and shaped," he explained to an interviewer as he neared seventy.

Stegner recalled the Eastend of his childhood as a polyglot mix of Texas and Montana cowboys, Cockneys from another Eastend across the Atlantic, Scandinavian newcomers like his mother up from North Dakota, and a sprinkling of Jews, Greeks, Syrians, and Chinese ranged in that order of community acceptance. Like DeVoto before him, Stegner, from the outset, sought to recover a Western past that had been obscured and nearly obliterated by the mythmakers and "the shoot-'em-up writers." "To take that real past and make some continuity between it and the real present is, I suppose, an ambition of mine," he explained in later characterizing his work.

Stegner's Eastend—or Whitemud, the fictional name he gave to the town—found its identity in an indestructible belief in a second chance as it was confronted by the equally unalterable fact of failure. The town collected failures by the dozens—hacks and has-beens, losers, "every sort of migrant, hopechaser, roughneck, trickster, incompetent, misfit, and failure." The town doctor was a suicidal alcoholic, the itinerant dentist a bumbling puller of teeth. Pop Martin, ranchman turned real estate developer and would-be local benefactor, was the victim of a string of natural catastrophes, including droughts, floods, and blizzards, which slowly whittled him away. But the most telling example of failure sabotaging schemes for making a quick buck was Stegner's own father, who finally learned the hard way "what the Plains settler could not learn, short of living it out . . . that no system of farming, no matter how strenuously applied, could produce crops in that country during one of the irregular and unpredictable periods of drought and that the consequence of trying to force the issue could be disastrous to both people and land."

In 1915 George Stegner decided to plunge by taking up a 360-acre homestead almost exactly on the international line and growing wheat, which was bringing sky-high wartime prices in both Canada and the United States. His plot of arid prairie lay two days by lumber wagon, one by buckboard from town across open land gullied by washouts and pockmarked by sloughs—hawk country, his son remembered, "all flickertails, prairie dogs, badgers, and gopher snakes," wholly unsuited for plowing, a fact that eluded the elder Stegner for five seasons. Acknowledging the natural limits placed on the land would have denied George his dream of quick profits which drove him so mercilessly that first year. Wallace recalled that his father took immense pride in plowing a six-inch furrow straight as a string for almost a mile. "He started at our pasture fence, plowed straight south to the line, turned east, plowed a few rods along the border, and turned north again to our fence, enclosing a long narrow field that in a demonic burst of non-stop work he plowed and disked and harrowed and planted to Red Fife wheat."

The Stegners made a big crop that first summer, and on the strength of it seeded another sixty acres the following year. A gambler's mistake, as it turned out, and the first betrayal of hope. The next year was too wet, and rust ruined the entire crop. There followed a series of blistering hot summers without rain—1917, 1918, 1919—which turned the fields to dust by mid-July. "My father did not grow discouraged; he grew furious. When he matched himself against something he wanted a chance to win." A year later, George took his family down to Montana and another sure thing, running bootleg whiskey in and out of Great Falls, "and we had stopped walking the paths and making our marks on the face of the prairie." "If" was the operative word for George Stegner and his neighbors: "If only". . . if only there hadn't been a drought. But there *was* a drought, and it taught a hard lesson: wheat farming beyond the 100th Meridian was a fool's errand bound to end badly. It was failure the Stegner family was living—"more than a family failure . . . it was the failure of a system and a dream. . . . This was where a mass human movement dwindled to its end."

Following a brief stay in Great Falls, George Stegner moved his family once again, this time to Salt Lake City and a succession of outposts across the city from which he conducted his guerrilla war against Prohibition. Throughout the twenties the Stegners moved all over town—from creaking bungalow to seedy apartment to a crumbling adobe near the post office. Wallace remembered Salt Lake City as an easy town to know, a systematically arranged sanctuary in which a person couldn't get lost. "That is much. And you can always see where you are. That is even more. And you can get clear up above the city and look all the way around it and over it, and that is most." Knowing Salt Lake City meant knowing its canyons, and like DeVoto a decade earlier and forty miles to the north, Stegner hiked them from the outskirts of downtown through lucerne fields and hanging meadows and orchards to the foot of arid benches and the peaks beyond.

Aridity, Stegner agreed with DeVoto and would continue to insist for the rest of his life, has always been a difficult fact of life for go-getting Americans to accept. But for those Westerners like

Wallace Stegner coming out of "deeply lived places" like Eastend and a failed homestead, aridity was a lesson you carried away and worked into all of your writing as he did in an early novel *On a Darkling Plain* (1940) and innumerable later essays. It was aridity and its sharp reminder of the limits nature had imposed on the West that linked Stegner and DeVoto in a shared outlook and a deep and lasting friendship as they began to educate Americans in the meaning of that fact. Another link between the two was a failed early novel that attempted unsuccessfully to transform this lesson into fiction.

Writing *On a Darkling Plain*, a work Stegner subsequently dismissed as "jejune," taught him the artistic limits of the free-floating imagination. Like DeVoto's *The Crooked Mile*, Stegner's novel is dominated by a stock character, Vickers, a weary and cynical war veteran scarred in mind and body but made whole again by the redeeming love of a young girl whose death in the flu epidemic, which devastates the town, returns him to the grieving community of survivors. The flu epidemic was real enough for the author, having wiped out nearly half the town of Eastend in 1919, but the story itself is formulaic, and its protagonist stereotypical. "The trouble with the book," confessed Stegner later, "and there's plenty of trouble with it, is that it's entirely *made*. It's an imagined novel, and war heroes I knew not one damned thing about. I knew nothing about war. . . . So the experiences of this character Vickers are purely hypothetical, disastrously so, I would say."

What is real and compelling in his flawed experiment is the prairie itself—the empty quarter where his hero seeks escape from the world. After days of unrelenting heat with the wind like an oven blast, the rain finally comes in a baptismal scene that the author himself must have frequently experienced:

Then one afternoon Vickers awoke from his nap wet with perspiration to find the air around him still, humid, suffocating, and lightning flickering in the cloud-piled east. A wind stirred. Out of the south a funnel of whirlwind raced across the prairie, lifting from the ground, dipping again, rearing and striking like an insane animal. Then the stir of dust of the yard again, an east wind this time, and in a split second the rain.

Standing in the doorway of his shack, Stegner's figure watches "the slant rain pour down, slicking the packed earth before his house, puddling in the shallow burnouts, running over the grass roots alive with movement, the air lovely and washed with the smell of drenched dust in it."

Limited literary achievements both, DeVoto's and Stegner's first novels are nevertheless filled with wide-lens landscapes—empty prairies, broad sweeps, receding horizons, gravel washes, shadowed canyons, deep gorges, and sheer peaks—whose overwhelming reality derives from their authors' felt experience. And as if to correct their declared intentions, their fictional forays were pointing both men toward the writing of *history* in their search for a usable Western past.

DeVoto and Stegner—"Benny" and "Wally," as they soon called each other—consolidated their friendship at the Bread Loaf Writers Conference held each summer for two frantic weeks on Bread Loaf Mountain near Middlebury College in Vermont. When Stegner joined his new friend and the fiction group in 1938, DeVoto had been a regular on the staff for most of the decade. Bread Loaf was designed for professionals—publishers, editors, and academicians as well as novelists, poets, dramatists, and historians who expected to publish and wanted their work to sell. Staff members included at one time or another Edward Weeks of the *Atlantic*,

Lovell Thompson of Houghton Mifflin, Herbert Agar of the Louisville *Courier-Journal,* and such visitors as the popular historians Fletcher Pratt and Catherine Drinker Bowen, novelists John Marquand and Hervey Allen, drama critics John Mason Brown and Walter Prichard Eaton, and poets Robert Hillyer and John Ciardi, the entire entourage presided over by the spirit and prickly presence of Robert Frost. From the beginning of the Bread Loaf sessions Stegner was attracted to Frost, whose poetry he greatly admired, while DeVoto's falling-out with the poet began with his discovery that Frost had a perverse side that enjoyed hurting people.

Stegner, a newcomer in 1938, came over from Greensboro and his new summer place, taking a break from repairing a ramshackle farmhouse and barn which, together with 200 acres of upland pasture and woods, he and Mary had just bought. Later he described Bread Loaf as a cross between Plato's Academy and *Walpurgisnacht*—immensely stimulating but totally exhausting. Throughout the thirties the conference was a haven for DeVoto, a gathered community of hard-driving professionals like him who spent long days given over to matters of craft and theory and spent their nights gossiping and carousing. Treman Cottage, home to the fiction staff, furnished scenes which both Stegner and DeVoto remembered vividly. Eudora Welty lounging at the feet of Katherine Anne Porter, deep in discussion of the modern short story. Carson McCullers listening attentively to W.H. Auden expound on poetic form. Also poker and improvised games of darts against the kitchen door with ice picks. And, late in the festivities, barbershop singing with voices well lubricated with liquor. There was also their joint memory of the beginnings of the breach between DeVoto and Robert Frost when the poet, who brooked no rivals, intentionally broke up an evening poetry reading by Archibald MacLeish by touching off a handful of newspapers while lighting his pipe and then violently fanning the flames. Later in Treman Cottage when MacLeish was prevailed upon to read from his new verse play *Air Raid*, Frost interrupted with wisecracks and caustic asides that grew more and more hostile until DeVoto could stand it no longer. "For God's sake, Robert," he insisted, "let him read." It was at the end of that summer's session that DeVoto parted from Frost with this memorable comment: "You're a good poet, Robert, but you're a bad man."

To their mutual acquaintances, DeVoto's and Stegner's friendship seemed a case of the attraction of opposites. In his younger colleague DeVoto found an impressive literary talent but also a steadier temperament and a more sanguine view of the world than he himself enjoyed. Stegner appeared forthright and sensible but also thoughtful and gentle. Where DeVoto reveled in controversy, Stegner scrupulously avoided it. Where DeVoto frequently blustered and bellowed, Stegner spoke with quiet conviction and authority. Yet both were sons of the Mountain West, intimately familiar with its landscape and arid climate, its history real and mythical. And both were consummate realists and ambitious professionals, teaching when the opportunity arose and meanwhile free-lancing with novels, stories, and articles to support work on the larger task of writing their region's history.

Stegner discerned in his friend a personality divided down the middle between public and private selves. There was DeVoto the boisterous performer—the last angry man—hiding his insecurity and feelings of inadequacy behind a calculated bluster and braggadocio, always outspoken and loud, often profane and not infrequently foul-mouthed. Here stood the self-made mythic Westerner—tough, no-nonsense, irreverent but realistic, a master of the facts and an enemy to pretenders. This was the DeVoto lampooned by a friend in a sketch for the conference newspaper as "the only live volcano in Vermont" and the "Ferocious Utah mountain lion, 'Ad hoc' tearing an author to bits."

There was another DeVoto, however, that Stegner soon discovered: a private, isolated, and lonely self in need of emotional support and willing to give it himself. The advice he dispensed to Stegner and other historian friends was intended and received as encouragement and appreciation even though his critical comments invariably hit their target. Frequently they concluded with the suggestion to "run it through the typewriter one more time." This helpful honesty Stegner recognized as the mark of the true professional who worked and lived by a code he himself professed. The "pro" knew that literature was art but also a business, and that it had finally to pay its way. This meant, as DeVoto explained, that the writer was constantly under the obligation "by skill and cunning to make contact with an audience." And this intent, in turn, meant reaching out to a variety of readers in a number of different ways and refusing to narrow one's professional horizon to clique or coterie. Stegner, for his part, needed no convincing.

Then too, both men were what DeVoto called apprentice New Englanders particularly partial to Vermont, whose people they admired and whose landscape in the rugged middle ground they responded to instinctively. In a moment of perception Stegner recognized his friend's love of Vermont as his own as well. "Though he does not seem to have said it anywhere, what he found exhilarating in Vermont was an extension into contemporary times of everything he admired about the frontier, as well as much that he had been familiar with from childhood."

Yet DeVoto, as Stegner came to understand, was "never at home in his home" but always in need of companionship for the settling of his restless soul. "Is there anywhere on your place," he asked after learning of Stegner's Greensboro farm, "where a man can walk—walk a long way, off the roads, in the woods?" And in Cambridge there would come desperate calls from DeVoto with demands that his friend "walk me around Fresh Pond." Here, perhaps, was an artist given to neurotic self-doubt and in constant need of propping up, but also a friend fundamentally affectionate and "utterly loyal"—"there have been few people to whom friendship meant more," Stegner recalled.

IV ⤳

The legacy bequeathed to DeVoto and Stegner took the form of a Western paradox composed of paired opposites: endless space and confining place; openings and barriers; belonging and rootlessness; opportunity and limits; freedom and constraint; dream and fact. The legacy came as a lesson in aridity which DeVoto described as marking "the end of a historic process" and Stegner as a permanent "condition of deficiency" lying beyond the 100th meridian. DeVoto would spend the fifteen years after 1940 seeking an underlying unity in the contradictory and conflicting Wests his meticulous research uncovered. He found that unity in what he called the "simple arithmetic" of scanty rainfall in a "grudging land" and a defiant topography. To his skeptical academic colleague, the chronicler of Manifest Destiny, Frederick Merk, he posed two questions designed to meet Merk on his own particularist ground. Why did most of the Oregon emigrants from the East go through South Pass? And why did the Oregon Trail follow the route that it did from the forks of the Platte to the Snake River? Such questions had, in De Voto's mind, unambiguous answers:

The answer to the first one is approximately: because there was only one other route across the Continental Divide that wagons could use, Marias Pass, and that was blocked with snow most of the travel season, and was exposed to Blackfeet besides. The answer to the other, besides South Pass, is roughly: because horses and oxen needed grass and they and the men needed water, had to go where the water and the grass were.

Here were those hard "facts" DeVoto had always insisted on commanding but with a difference now. Now he was after larger generalizations—verifying, for example, Lincoln's prediction that the West would be home to a single national family. In envisioning the trans-Mississippi West as the place where the nation would finally be completed, DeVoto declared, Lincoln spoke "the literal truth, literal as all hell." In this sense geography determined destiny, and in DeVoto's newly acquired patriotic view, geography determined the nation's Manifest Destiny—a conclusion he had reached with the approach of another world war. All three of his great histories would proceed from a conviction that there was indeed an underlying pattern, not simply to Western, but to a larger national history as well. And that pattern was first traced across the forbidding landscape of the West. Geography made the trails and determined the routes running westward through rising foothills to badland haunted by mirages, up steepening grades to mountains filled with crazy gullies and boulder-strewn canyons, swift-running rivers and up again to snow-covered peaks and precipitous descents to Oregon or California. Or the trail ran southwest from Independence down into empty desert country which ended suddenly in green valleys and sprawling ranches outside Santa Fe, home of an ancient culture awaiting American invigoration. "I am perfectly willing to forgo the word 'history,'" he told the doubting Frederick Merk, "and say that I'm not writing history, if that will help. But it seems only a quibble, for I make no judgments outside the area of historical facts, and, I believe, I say nothing that I cannot fully establish."

For DeVoto it was primarily the physical conformation of the High Plains and Rocky Mountains which shaped the behavior of the diverse peoples who crossed them or settled there. For Wallace Stegner, wrestling with the same problem of environmental influence, Western difference was "more than topography and landforms, dirt and rock." It was also climate as "atmosphere, flora, fauna." Aridity, he was convinced, and "aridity alone makes the various Wests one."

> The distinctive western plants and animals, the hard clarity (before power plants and metropolitan traffic altered it) of the western air, the look and location of western towns, the empty spaces that separate them, the way farms and ranches are deeply concentrated where water is plentiful or widely scattered where it is scarce, the pervasive presence of the federal government as land owner and land manager, the even more noticeable federal presence as dam builder and water broker, the snarling states' rights and antifederal feeling . . . those are all consequences . . . of aridity.

By 1940 DeVoto's *The Year of Decision: 1846* had already taken final shape in his mind. Its central theme, he was now sure, was the impress of the West as initiatory rite in the creation of an American mind and character, the making of a patriot people out of its land and the tests of endurance it demanded. It was Stegner's complementary conviction born of memories of the scorched prairies his father had tried to farm and reinforced by adolescent summers on the Plateau Province of southern Utah that determined him to tackle his biography of John Wesley Powell, one of the West's original culture heroes who spent an entire career trying to teach Americans the limits imposed by dry land.

Stegner and DeVoto's shared legacy in the coming years would bind them, first as working historians and then as engaged environmental activists, to the task of teaching their fellow citizens how to understand the American land and how to care for it. As a fellow practitioner of popular history Stegner understood instinctively that in recasting past events as personal experience, asserting the historian's constant presence, and "converting chronology into simultaneity" in *The Year of Decision: 1846* DeVoto "was doing something no American historian had done." A few years later, as Stegner struggled with *Beyond the Hundredth Meridian*, his biography of John Wesley Powell, DeVoto reciprocated with an admiring letter and advice to make the most of his superb descriptive power. "Everything you say about the background of deprivation here will earn you from ten to a thousand later on," adding in the margins "Esp. the Arid Region."

What, then, were readers of their histories, those confident and go-getting Americans, to do with this legacy of limits? Stegner spoke for both men in answering the question. "You may deny it for a while. Then you must try to engineer it out of existence or adapt to it." Which accommodation both writers had made long ago, having understood more or less exactly the nature of the inheritance left them by their origin and the obligation to make environmental history out of it. The environmental history both men were already writing as the nation emerged victorious from the Second World War was not intended for academicians and trained specialists but for the common reader with a taste for romantic adventure and monumental scenery, grand spectacle and heroic undertakings. Theirs would be history as a form of art for all Americans. This history would necessarily be the story of their home country, its exploration, settlement, development, and imminent degradation. The terrain would be regional, but their message and its intended audience in a new age of environmental exploitation would be national.

History

Overleaf: View of Marble Canyon from Vermilion Cliffs. (From *The Exploration of the Colorado River and Its Canyons*, J. W. Powell, 1895.)

I ⌁

It was history and the Harvard history department that Bernard DeVoto missed most when in the spring of 1936 he was denied tenure and moved to New York, a city he loathed, to breathe new life into the ailing *Saturday Review of Literature* while at the same time holding forth from *Harper's* "Easy Chair". Abandoning Cambridge and Boston for suburban White Plains and a frenzied midtown Manhattan meant saying goodbye "to all that is left of the eighteenth century" and issuing a surly greeting to a city "where the applied ingenuity of mankind has striven to outdo the hideousness of a rathole and succeeded." He spent more than a year at the *Saturday Review* trying to revive it by parceling out assignments to his friends and former Harvard colleagues Samuel Eliot Morison, Paul Buck, and Arthur Schlesinger, Sr., and recruiting new talent from his Bread Loaf circle. His own contributions to both magazines rehearsed all his old prejudices, and his style continued to display a patented belligerence and personal animus. His enemies also remained the same—misguided Marxists, literary nay-sayers, pedagogical pietists, and various and sundry "neomaniacs" stalking the journalistic halls of the city. "Every literary movement that ever existed," he announced on arrival, "has been infested with such vegetarians, dew-walkers, numerologists, and swamis." He intended to take on all of them.

The New York interlude also saw a further broadening of DeVoto's already catholic cultural concerns. Given free rein, his imagination ranged widely across America in time and space—from the Lewis and Clark expedition to the unintended consequences of the Civil War, from the New England hurricane of 1938 as a foreshadowing of the coming devastation of World War II to a bemused observer's rankings of post-Christmas academic conventions, bestowing ironic accolades on the sociologists as the windiest and funniest and dismissing the Modern Language Association's conclave as the dreariest and "most fretful." Insisting that he was a mere journalist following his curiosity wherever it took him, in reality he was training himself as a pioneer popular historian with a growing appreciation of other practitioners like Mari Sandoz and Catherine Drinker Bowen, and as a student of popular culture with a lively interest in the work of Constance Rourke and Gilbert Seldes's irreverent treatment of academic high seriousness. Culture, he realized, was both broader and deeper than books, more vital and variegated. "Culture" was a word for all seasons and climes, but it was most fruitfully employed with the prefix "a" to avoid absolutes and include interests and pursuits unacknowledged by systematic literary pundits. Culture, properly understood, was inevitably *popular* culture, and the historian who sought to comprehend it was a *popular* historian.

Whatever the topic under scrutiny in DeVoto's columns and essays he continued to approach it with his long-standing bias against what he called "systems" and "gospel." Both fed a hankering for authority and absolutism which ensnared the unwary individual. And it was the individual, he had known all along, with whom he was primarily concerned. "What interests me," he explained to the puzzled critic Edmund Wilson, who had inquired into the nature of DeVoto's beliefs, "is primarily the human emotions and experiences that have only a secondary connection with social movements. . . . My absorption is men and women in relationships which are immediately human but are economic only at many removes or at infinity." Marx's economic determinism simply built another closed system whose inhabitants look at their master's map of the present and future and accept it so completely that "where Marx says a mountain or a molehill must be found, they find it whether it is there or not." As for capitalist democracy and the middle class, neither was on the road to extinction. "You may prophesy," he told Wilson, "but I will not. I hear the voice of lamentation but it is past noon and no fire has come. Peradventure Marx sleepeth and must be awaked."

In announcing his bourgeois prejudices DeVoto frequently lapsed into autobiography as he did in his exchange with Edmund Wilson. He had not intended to become a writer, he explained, and had been urged by his father to consider mineralogy. But when the crystallographic cardboard models seemed to bear no relationship to real rocks, he gave up on the project. His decision to cast himself as a public intellectual nevertheless rested on a strong if simplistic appreciation of hard science which theorized only on the basis of facts, observations, operations, and evidence. This analytical process the literary left could not or would not perform, preferring instead to rely on Marx's self-proclaimed "truths." What the left theorists failed to realize was that "a machine gun is set up at the core of every higher truth thus revealed, and that it is dangerous to let even a generous man get his hands on a machine gun." DeVoto's long-standing fear of totalitarianism in all its forms grew sharper as the war crisis in Europe intensified.

By the end of 1937 it was clear that the *Saturday Review*'s circulation problems were not responding to DeVoto's heroic therapy, and he was given three months' notice. Back in Cambridge with his family and furnished office in Harvard's Widener Library, he continued to edit the Mark Twain Papers under the disapproving eye of Twain's overly protective daughter whose frequent complaints made his task difficult. De Voto's family (Mark, a second son, was born in 1940) eventually settled in a house on Cambridge's Berkeley Street where in his closely guarded study De Voto began writing history.

Cut loose from Harvard, DeVoto still retained close intellectual friendships with the members of the history department, and in the English department, with Kenneth Murdock, veteran teacher and former dean of the faculty who served as a loyal supporter and steadying personal influence. In addition there were Samuel Eliot Morison, Perry Miller, and Arthur Schlesinger, Sr., with whom DeVoto had planned Harvard's new program in American civilization. All of these former colleagues, while occasionally wary of DeVoto's outspoken manner, were fully appreciative of his broad definition of American culture, which was already transforming the teaching of progressive history. He also kept up connections with Columbia historians Henry Steele Commager and Garrett Mattingly, his former colleague at Northwestern, with whom he remained intellectually very close. Mattingly, the author of a superb narrative history of the defeat of the Spanish Armada in 1588, continued to supply DeVoto with lengthy letters of advice and appreciation of his sweeping narrative style.

In New York the editorial fraternity at *Harper's* also furnished a sustaining collegiality, in particular Jack Fisher, John Kouwenhoven, Russell Lynes and the rest of the "Sixth Floor Front" as DeVoto called them in dedicating a collection of his "Easy Chair" pieces to them in 1955. All of these friends were themselves critics and commentators who published lively analyses of American culture, both folk and popular, vernacular and formal. All of them shared DeVoto's concern with politics and the arts, and patiently endured his abrasive style in the hope of enlightenment, however rudely delivered. Add to this list of Eastern intellectuals a growing number of Western environmental writers and watchdogs whose reports on the state of the land beyond the Mississippi DeVoto counted on in launching his attacks on predatory grazing interests.

By 1940, when he headed west with young Arthur Schlesinger, Jr., on an inspection tour, DeVoto was part of the broad circle of American independent intellectuals like Edmund Wilson and Mary McCarthy on the left and Lewis Mumford and Van Wyck Brooks on the regionalist right—critics and commentators poised at the edges of academia but as yet unattached to it as sharp observers of the American scene. That scene, in the summer of 1940, was being played out on the contested ground of American involvement in the European crisis.

As the crisis in Europe deepened and Germany began assembling its war machine for the invasion of Poland and Russia, DeVoto, who had been following events on the continent apprehensively, now warned publicly of the dangers of neutrality and isolationism. In an "Easy Chair" piece for November 1939 entitled "The Oncoming," he compared his feelings with those of a younger self twenty-five years earlier when a romantic adolescent in Ogden, Utah, dreamed of a distant storybook war fought with derring-do by selfless patriots. "This time," he warned, "it will be neither distant nor romantic." When the United States entered the First World War, he remembered enlisting enthusiastically after catching "a swift, brief glimpse of a nation that has never quite existed." Then it had been the bulletin board in front of Ogden's newspaper office that served as a young patriot's source of information. Now hundreds of radio voices announced the end of "a kind of peace" and the enactment of war powers acts by England and France. Americans, DeVoto realized, remained sharply divided on the nature of their national interests, the dangers of fascism and communism, and the wisdom of a policy of neutrality. He himself approved heartily of the interventionist spirit that he saw surging across the country. "There will be, for a while, more *we* in America than there has been," he assured readers, predicting that "America will wage war in one way or another and take the responsibility of fitting together what fragments of the world are left when it is finished." Once again as in 1917 there was a "misty glimpse" of Woodrow Wilson's world made safe for democracy except that then it was a mere "pleasant promise" while "here is payday." His nine-year-old son Gordon asked him why there was war if war was so terrible. What to answer? "Tell him that my boyhood too had the promise of peace in it. . . . Tell him that all boyhoods have the promise of peace." His son would not grow up in an America he was born in, "but neither did I or anyone else . . . and if he cannot have the hope perhaps he can have the will to do more than I did in the shaping of America. . . . To save what we can and make what we can of what is saved." Although he could not yet measure the lengths the postwar task of protecting the environment would carry him, already he sensed the nature of the challenge.

The premonitory piece was the first of some two dozen essays and articles, first on the likelihood of American involvement, then on the waging of the war and the problems of the ensuing peace which DeVoto would compose while finishing *The Year of Decision: 1846*. Together the completed manuscript and the war essays marked a turning of his mind away from angry debates on the standards for literature and the nature of culture to the forging of American nationalism and the making of an American people. That initial act of creation, he had known for some time, occurred as the nation approached its middle years in the nineteenth century. It took place in the Great West as adventurous emigrants from the East made their various ways across the High Plains and over the mountains to the Great Valley and on to Oregon and California. This was the story he proceeded to tell in *The Year of Decision: 1846*, a saga designed, as he explained in the preface, "to realize the pre-Civil War Far Western frontier as personal experience."

The opening years of the Second World War saw the completion of the first volume of DeVoto's magisterial history of the West, but its conception had come ten years earlier. He had written in the Depression summer of 1933 to Garrett Mattingly, then at Columbia, to report progress on his frontier trilogy—"tetralogy?"—"polyogy?"—or perhaps "teratology?" He was going "to isolate the frontier bacillus by selecting a year when it was most in evidence and describing that year as completely as possible." He would need a national stage and a cast of thousands, most of them following their destinies along river courses, up arid plateaus, over deserts, and across mountains. Such a grand design would require "as much marching and counter-marching as possible, hullabaloo, off-stage noises, red fire, wind machines, and sidereal auroras." True to his promise, DeVoto opened his story of that year with the appearance of Biela's comet on its seven-year perihelion passage in January of the year of decision.

Early in the planning of his history of a year DeVoto realized that he would also need what he called a "culture hero," a witness to the transformation of American democratic society, a representative common man whose life crossed the divide between East and West and between republic and empire. He found his man in Jim Clyman, fur trapper and mountain man turned guide to the emigrant trains which were changing his way of life irrevocably. "Look at his career," he urged Mattingly and then proceeded to rehearse it for him. Born in George Washington's Virginia and met the old general as a young boy. Present at Tippecanoe and served in the militia in the War of 1812. Joined the Ashley fur traders, roamed the Mountain West, and explored the Great Salt Lake. Five years as a trapper and then back to the Old Northwest and brief military service again, this time in the Blackhawk War. Tried farming for a spell in Wisconsin, shot by the Winnebagoes, harassed by Blackfeet. Member of the first Oregon emigration in 1844, then of the Applegate Party to California where he met John C. Fremont and took part in the abortive Black Flag Revolt. Then back east once more and another series of journeys through the mountains. Arrived at Sutters Mill in time to see gold discovered. Finally married, settled down in Napa Valley, and died halfway through the administration of Rutherford B. Hayes. "Think that career over," DeVoto told Mattingly a decade before Clyman was reincarnated in the pages of *The Year of Decision*. "And I didn't invent a comma of it." Clyman's life defined precisely the transition of the nation from Jeffersonian republic to world power. Yet like DeVoto's Mormon grandfather, Clyman was an unwitting instrument of forces he scarcely understood. He helped open the Great West and then exploited it mercilessly for a pittance paid by the fur monopoly, changed jobs when the trade played out, and guided his fellow countrymen along the trails he knew by heart to their various destinations. When DeVoto told Edmund Wilson that for him history consisted of the stories of individuals, it was the likes of Jim Clyman he had in mind. Wallace Stegner, who greatly admired his friend's storytelling prowess, recognized the novelistic use of the culture hero as synecdoche, a device for compressing and compacting meaning. "Sample. Symbol. Culture hero. A part that might be taken for the whole, an individual in whose experience was subsumed a whole folk-wandering."

American entry into World War II coincided with the completion of *The Year of Decision,* which DeVoto finished in February

1942. The book was serialized that same year in the *Atlantic Monthly*, selected by the Book-of-the-Month-Club, and appeared in the bookstores in March 1943. By that time the author was deeply involved in the war effort. The war brought all of DeVoto's latent patriotism to the surface as he joined with thousands of intellectuals and academics who flocked to Washington to offer their services. He was never called, although late in the war he held abortive discussions with the War Department concerning a project for a series of histories of major military campaigns from Guadalcanal to North Africa. His enthusiasm waned and plans were ultimately abandoned when he learned that he would not be given access to battle reports or the confidential papers of the participants. The setback ended his hopes for contributing directly to an American victory but only strengthened his determination to sit in judgment in the "Easy Chair" and issue warnings against isolationism and complacency, finding precedents for patriotic sacrifice in the Civil War, and above all railing against government censorship and the withholding of information vital to citizen morale. His insistence on the people's right to know, forcefully asserted throughout the war, would be quickly transferred to domestic affairs and national resource management in the postwar years. And by then it would be clear that he had fashioned out of his war experiences and his historical writing a political philosophy of participatory populist nationalism resting on an informed and involved citizenry educated in democratic values, cognizant of limits, and wary of policymakers. The possibility of implementing this democratic national creed awaited the winning of the war, but the original creation of an American nationalism and the actual making of a nation, as he had learned in the process of writing his history, was the achievement of America's Manifest Destiny in the year of decision a century earlier.

In all of his histories DeVoto was absorbed with matters of form. "I still know as little as ever and I'm oppressed by it," he confided to Mattingly as he struggled with the third volume of his projected trilogy. "But also I'm suddenly oppressed by how much I know, at least how much information I have, and how hard it's going to be to impose form on it and make it readable. I suppose there is a structure; I know it's going to be hell to find it." By "form" and "structure" DeVoto, and in his turn Wallace Stegner, meant a workable strategy that would give their history a brisk pace, narrative drive, and a personally felt meaning. DeVoto's particular problem stemmed from his conviction that real history lies outside books and literary pronouncements in those myriad cultural "facts" his research kept turning up. "The realities of the American past," he had written ten years before the appearance of *The Year of Decision*, "refuse to form coherent sequences, being full of contradictions, disparate elements, eccentric and disruptive forces that war with one another, events and tendencies and personalities that cannot be reduced to a formula." Those damnable little facts, puzzling and often inconsistent, could make writing history a living hell. "I am not going to join you any longer," he announced to his confessor Garrett Mattingly in a recurrent mood of feigned despair, "in the pretense that I have the kind of mind that can write history. . . . I am quite incapable of determining facts, recognizing facts, appraising facts, putting facts in relation to one another, confining myself to facts, guiding myself by facts, or even recording facts. My mind is an instrument superbly designed for inaccuracy." Such posturing aside, DeVoto realized upon reflection that the form he sought for his history involved transforming these facts through an act of literary imagination. His own imagination led him directly to the use of two literary techniques: synecdoche, the compressing of the disparate *many* into the representative *one*; and simultaneity, the multiple drama-tizing of several courses of action occurring at the same time. These two devices drive DeVoto's account of the year 1846.

Managing all of these facts also required a constant authorial presence as storyteller, arranging his material, pointing out its significance, commenting, criticizing, dismissing as he goes along. Wallace Stegner explained his friend's use of the personal point of view approvingly. "DeVoto did not want to be off some-where like the God of creation, indifferent, paring his fingernails. He was a positive man with positive opinions, and he must have liked the sense that as historian he had no need to hide or dis-guise either his attitudes or his personal gift for language." Both DeVoto and Stegner discovered in the nineteenth-century romantic historian Francis Parkman the transformative power of fictional techniques employed for factual purposes in composing history not as record but drama. Not many of DeVoto's academic colleagues approved or even understood his clever use of these devices. Trained in the progressive history methods of assumed objectivity, they continued to preach to their students the virtues of scientific accuracy, dispassionate distance, and chaste prose— just the sort of history that DeVoto and Stegner rejected and sometimes ridiculed.

In *The Year of Decision* he found his form. The book was received and read, as he intended it to be, as an artful piece of synecdoche condensing into a single year the story of the national transit from Old Republic to New Empire, at once a romantic celebration of heroism and perfidy and a vast verbal map of the entire country crisscrossed by tortuous trails, emigrant trains, armies on the march, commercial agents and political promoters of Manifest Destiny. More than a literary experiment, the book was also a com-pacted account of its author's understanding of history, a guide to

Western topography and climate, and a rich and provocative reading of American culture.

DeVoto's vast terrain with its successive ordeals required representative figures to experience it and dominate or succumb to it. He filled his landscape with a wide selection of types. In Transcendental New England, for which the author had slight sympathy, there is Fruitland's orphic Bronson Alcott mouthing "noble drool" while his wife and children did all the work. Along the Santa Fe Trail, the young bride of an old trader, Susan Magoffin, suffers a miscarriage and other discomforts. "Owl" Russell, ex-Kentucky colonel and deposed captain of a wagon train, lectures Francis Parkman while solacing his wounded pride with white lightning. Then there is Ethan Allen Hitchcock, unsung commissary general to the inept Zachary Taylor, inaccurately named "Old Rough and Ready," and Thomas O. Larkin, the capable American consul in Monterey managing his country's interests quietly and adroitly. These and dozens of other figures served DeVoto as walk-ons in his unfolding drama.

In addition to his "culture hero," Jim Clyman, bearer of common virtue, DeVoto also needed a presiding genius, and this he discovered in the great organizer and Mormon leader Brigham Young, propelled westward to the Great Valley by a strange but powerful religion. In place of Jim Clyman's sharply honed instinct for survival, Brigham, a superb if autocratic manager of men, substituted a faith in the collective salvation of his people and an unshakable conviction of divine authority vested in himself. It is Brigham who decides that an advanced party be dispatched to the Great Basin to prepare the way. And Brigham once more who sees the need to set up in the valley before the Gentiles arrive and thus understands the urgency of volunteering a Mormon Battalion to help defeat the Mexicans even though it means telling the reluctant enlistees that they must now love the government that had thrown them out. Off they go with Brigham's instructions to "be humble, teach charity, eschew profanity." Meanwhile he stipulates to the federal government the costs of the Saints' support: "Israel needed wagons, stock, supplies, clothing, money, and if the Lord pleased to provide them by government subsidy, Brigham could see the joke." Despite DeVoto's curt dismissal of Mormonism itself, no other hero in his collection is more clearly marked with authorial grace than Brigham Young.

Confronting DeVoto's heroes stand the pretenders and charlatans who range from the harmless "smock-wearers" preaching the "newest Newness" in Eastern communitarian experiments to genuinely despicable con men like the commercial promoter Lansford Hastings whose book advertising a shortcut to California he had never traveled costs the Donner Party their lives. Hastings compounds his culpability in a letter to emigrants bound for California. His route across the desert to the Sierras, he tells them, is four hundred miles shorter than the Fort Hall trail, less mountainous, easier on the animals, and free of hostile Indians. "It is clear that he was not crazy," DeVoto comments, "so he was lying." To underscore the Mormons' achievement in gathering Zion under nearly prohibitive conditions DeVoto contrasts them with the well-meaning but hapless intellectuals sojourning at Brook Farm, forerunners, in the author's mind, of the coterie of New York intellectuals. The Brook Farmers are converts to "right development," but they are unwilling to carry out their principles. Refined passions and virtuous labor and perfect cooperation—all quite admirable! "Yet mortgages had to be paid, the brute lingered and the angel delayed, and the literary ended in despair." Literary folk love the people but despise the mob. Members of one another only on their own restrictive terms, the Brook Farmers lacked the passion and the fortitude needed to make a people and change the world. They needed a hotter fire than the one that consumed their Phalanstery. The Mormons, on the other hand, "were members of one another much more truly than Brook Farm—and may leave our history the moral that association needs the lowest common denominator."

The East holds no monopoly on literary pretension and social silliness. Western windiness blowing across the year of decision issues chiefly from the Pathfinder John C. Frémont, whom the author presently dubs "Childe Harold" after the Byronic model. Childe Harold is another man of many words and few deeds, a writer of letters to his adoring wife, a composer of endless ultimatums, and a perpetually frustrated seeker after glory. "Greatness was a burden on Childe Harold's soul but nature kept the lines a little out of drawing." As the year 1846 unfolds, Frémont's hour presumably arrives with the *opera buffa* Black Flag Revolt, and from there matters scarcely improve. Alas! "Nothing came out quite the way it should have done. Lord Byron, who had imagined him, could not make him rhyme."

DeVoto's portrait of the antihero darkens with the consequences for his victims. William Gilpin, former frontiersman turned gusty rhetorician and geopolitical prophet, trumpets the centrality of the High Plains in God's plan for the redemption of the world. Gilpin is another man of inspired prophecy but scant knowledge of his subject. Predicting boundless harvests and celestial railways, Gilpin committed the cardinal sin for which neither DeVoto nor, later, Wallace Stegner could forgive him—a repeated denial of aridity as the primary condition in Western life. Gilpin appears only briefly in *The Year of Decision*, but in an essay in *Harper's* that same year of publication entitled "Geopolitics With Dew On It," DeVoto lambasted him for his "a priori, deduced, generalized, falsely systematized, and therefore wrong" practice of science. Gilpin, he charged, looked down the Great Valley of the Mississippi from on high and beheld a huge amphitheater stretching from the Appalachians to the Rockies "ready to receive and fuse harmoniously whatever enters its rim." According to Gilpin the High Plains was not desert but the "OPPOSITE," the material base and spiritual center of the great nation of futurity. For their part DeVoto and, then at greater length, Stegner pronounced Gilpin's words pure fustian, full of misinformation and miscalculation that would cost would-be homesteaders dearly for the rest of the century.

DeVoto's own factual reach and personal interest did not extend to what a later age would call ethnic and gender pluralism or to issues concerning the cultural margins—of the whole West as a contested ground for Anglo-Saxons, Spanish, Mexicans, Native Americans, Asians, and women in all of these categories. Wallace Stegner compiled a damning report on American prejudice and racism for *Look* magazine in 1945, later published as *One Nation*, a pioneer exploration of cultural relativism and the urgent need for tolerance, which pointed the way to the sixties and beyond. But DeVoto was searching for a different kind of unity— a unifying patriotism as a civic religion to guide Americans in conducting their war against the Axis and fashioning a durable peace. DeVoto's sense of diversity was based primarily on region, class, and a European cultural inheritance, which is to say that in pledging his allegiance to the motto *e pluribus unum* his emphasis fell on the latter word. He fictionalized diversity in his emigrant everyman "Bill Bowen" hailing from all over the East—Maine to Georgia, Vermont to Illinois—drawn west by promise and representing a confluence of social and occupational types "poured into this retort, a complete democracy, all classes and conditions, background, moralities, philosophies, and culture." The mythical Bill Bowen's real-life counterparts include a Kentucky colonel, a Yankee editor, a former Missouri governor, and a well-to-do patriarch, George Donner, and his third wife, Tamsen, a level-headed young schoolmarm.

In their separate ways these and all the other emigrants undergo the ordeal of the trail, leaving Independence, the jumping-off point, as a "village on wheels, and the mind and habit of villages inclosed in it." Slowly at first and then more rapidly the disintegrative forces of topography and climate take their toll. Wagon trains split up, personal rivalries and animosities appear with the coming of frigid nights and cold breakfasts, lack of water and hidden quicksands, all working a "constant attrition on the nerves." "God Himself seemed hostile when there was added to them a bad storm or some neighbor's obstinacy that reacted to the common loss." The atomization of the village proceeds apace and intensifies as the emigrants experience the gradual extinction of everything familiar—"the unseen, steady seepage of the life you had been bred to." The land grew stranger and more threatening. "It had no bound; the long heave of the continent never found a limit, and in that waste the strongest personality diminished." Loneliness, dissociation, and all kinds of physical ailments took their toll. Some emigrants survived unscathed, but others were permanently scarred. "Worse country lay ahead and the drained mind was less able to meet it."

As the prairies give way to the High Plains, difficulties multiply. Oxen collapse and die from the heat. Old folks die from sheer fatigue and are buried in shallow graves. Diarrhea, nausea, piercing headaches—they called it "mountain fever," the result of bad water and thinning oxygen. Sagebrush and alkali country. Mirages, badlands, spectacular vistas but treacherous going. Hail Rock,

Courthouse Rock, Chimney Rock, Scott's Bluff—"eroded mon-strosities" and "individual items in creation's slag heap."

With a cartographer's precision DeVoto retraces the diverging routes and pauses to note their effects on the emigrants:

Beyond the Platte. . . .

The grade was steep now, and once they were in the badlands the trail narrowed and was frequently precipitous. Crazy gullies and canyons cut every which way, and whoever gave up in anger and tried to find better going elsewhere only found worse troubles. . . .

Deep in the Badlands. . . .

Ropes fray, wagons have to be pulled or lowered by hand. When they moved, the dry axles added a torturing shriek to the split-reed soprano of the wheels and the scrape of tires on stone or rubble. Dry air had shrunk the wheels, too, and without warning tires rolled off or spokes pulled out and the wagon stalled. . . .

Nearing South Pass and the Halfway Point. . . .

Add to the increasing strain the altitude making the nerves tauter. Though the violent sun was hot and the dust pall breathless, there were sudden viciously cold days too and the nights were cold. Water froze in the pails. . . . It was a triphammer, the test itself. . . .

With Susan Magoffin and her husband at Pawnee Fork on their way to Bent's Fort

. . . . and now the mosquitoes were worse than ever. They mad-dened the mules, when Susan stepped out into the grass her dress filled with them, at night they sounded like rain on the roof, and she was made sick by their stings. . . .

With the advance Harland-Young Party struggling through the Wasatch Mountains on Hastings Cutoff. . . .

They barely made it. Narrow, bush-choked, and boulder-filled canyons, precipitous divides, stretches many miles long of almost impenetrable brush, and above all the course of the Weber River between vertical mountain walls that rose straight from the water's edge. . . .

With the Donner Party in the Sierras. . . .

In that mound of snow, Graves's corpse upholding its part of the tent, they stayed all through Christmas Day, while the blizzard howled on and made the mound bigger. That morning delirium came upon Patrick Dolan and, screaming, he broke his way through tent and snow. Eddy went out into the blizzard and tried to bring him back but could not. He came back after a while, and they held him down till he sank into a coma. As dusk seeped through the blizzard, he died.

In 1846 the United States along with the thousands of emigrants heading west took a decisive turn. Though the great majority of Americans did not yet realize the fact, the addition of the Great West made the Civil War, the death of slavery, and the rise of a single continental nation inevitable. Lincoln had been right: one nation, one economic empire, one national consciousness. Slowly the United States, driven by the logic of geography, began to respond to new impulses and forces. In the future the lines of influence and power would run east and west instead of north and south. "The center of gravity had been displaced," as "the achieved West had given the United States something that no people had ever had before: an internal, domestic empire." A century later, that mature democratic empire was engaged in a war against a vicious totalitarianism, which DeVoto had consistently warned was the predictable result of closed ideological systems and exclusionist cultural theories.

Writing *The Year of Decision* in the midst of a world war nationalized DeVoto's perspective and politicized the man. His new domestic enemy resided in Washington in the person of the smug bureaucrat who always claimed to know better and constantly denied citizens needed information. DeVoto fought his own private war against the censors, their mismanagement and cynicism, from his desk at *Harper's*. He complained to his friend Elmer Davis, who had gone to Washington to head the Office of War Information. Davis, who was sympathetic, asked if he had a better idea. Indeed he did, he replied. He would begin by telling people what was happening and enlisting their support by asking their views. That was democracy. "You know God damned well that if we mean what we say by democracy, that's the first step." The way to create an informed public opinion was to begin by informing the public.

For DeVoto the wartime danger was not simply censorship but the apparent cynicism behind it masking as reason of state. The administration gave the lie to freedom of press by refusing to divulge and discuss its plans for the postwar world and future domestic policy in particular. "There is a hell of a lot more to it than information about the war and peace," he told Davis, adding, "I do believe that the New Deal has got tired, that it does not believe what it says, that it does not accept what I described as the democratic postulates." The New Deal, once the liberal interventionist manager of the American land, seemed in danger of losing its way. DeVoto was a devout democrat if an increasingly doubting Democrat with worries about the growth of executive power during the latter years of the Roosevelt administration. The only check on executive usurpation, he lectured Davis, was Congress, and though working with that institution was no easy task, "by God, Congress is part of the government we are committed to, and until that form is changed we have damned well got to work with it." Just how difficult that assignment was would soon become clear to him.

The germination of DeVoto's second volume in his trilogy of the West seemed routine and unspectacular. Early in 1944, having finished *The Year of Decision*, he was approached by a literary agent and sometime publisher with a bundle of more than one hundred watercolors by the nineteenth-century Baltimore artist of the West, Alfred Jacob Miller, who had accompanied the Scottish baronet Sir William Drummond Stewart on his seven-year tour of the West in the waning days of the fur trade in the late 1830s. At first, DeVoto was intrigued if noncommittal, but his vision of the project expanded rapidly as he discerned the outlines of a story of the passing of an entire age along with the tribe of mountain men who were at once its heroes and its captives. After considerable debate over the terms of the contract and an unpleasant exchange of letters with the holder of the artwork DeVoto managed to secure an agreement giving him the control he required. In February 1945 he set to work on what would become *Across the Wide Missouri*, a detailed account of the glory days and precipitous decline of the fur trade, in which Sir William Stewart and Miller had been participants and observers.

By the time DeVoto finished his account of the mountain men, what had originated as a potboiler had become a two-hundred-thousand-word saga. His insistence on accuracy and specificity was as strong as ever, and his frustration mounted when the maps in his Cambridge study afforded the only means of visualizing his landscape. He admitted his irritation in a letter to

Garrett Mattingly. "This morning I four times got up from my desk, and went to the map at the other end and looked up the direction of flow of the two forks of Snake River, then went back to my desk, found I'd written it down exactly wrong after walking a measured eighteen feet, and corrected it, and not liking the correction, went back to the map, etc. Four times, and after the fourth time I still had it exactly wrong." Precise placement mattered crucially to DeVoto because of his methods of composition, which he explained as "simultaneousness"—the technique of laying out and following several courses of action at the same time—and "test-boring"—the use of particular people and events to represent larger forces and encapsulate greater meaning. Again he used these two devices profusely in the attempt to encompass the whole of the Great West.

What Sir William Stewart witnessed and Jacob Miller recorded was the end of the fur trade in the decade before the coming of the migration to Oregon and California. From one angle the mountain men appeared magnificent examples of frontier hardihood and intrepidity, unsullied heroes living lives of total freedom. Yet from another they seemed prisoners of the fur monopolies, which exploited them mercilessly as they proceeded to destroy the beaver population. DeVoto's populist admiration for permanent settlers and the care they, like his grandfather Dye, lavished on the land helped him to recognize the fur monopolies as precursors of the extractive predators of a later day—cattle corporations, mining syndicates, lumber combines—laying waste to the region. Jim Clyman, Joe Meek, and Jim Bridger might have been marvels of bravery and endurance, but they were also unwitting or uncaring agents of environmental destruction. In one attitude they stood as legendary figures in a storied past, but in another as determined spoilers and pillagers unaware of their real historical role. This was precisely what DeVoto meant when he explained in his preface that he aimed to describe the fur trade "as a business and a way of life."

The book was also high drama—the work, Wallace Stegner observed, of a "spoiled novelist." DeVoto's story covers the decade of the 1830s during most of which Stewart and Miller were touring the Great West and encountering most of its transient inhabitants—trappers, Indians, traders, guides, and speculators. The scale is panoramic, the cast again one of thousands as the narrative crisscrosses the land along the trails it follows. Though he still considered himself a tolerably talented novelist, DeVoto agreed with Stegner in distinguishing his history from that written by academicians. "Very few historians of our time," he told an admirer from Ogden, "realize that history is not only knowledge, not only knowledge and wisdom even, but also art." His own books, he continued, employed the techniques and the structures of literature. "They have form." And that form embodied the meaning: it was "the end in view." Writing history this way was not an easy task because if properly constructed it read more like a novel than a monograph. This was something which academic historians failed to understand—the immensity and complexity of the past and the techniques needed to register it. History-making materials are "so multifarious," he explained to his correspondent, that they demand new approaches and methods. Which was precisely his intention in *Across the Wide Missouri* and its predecessor, *The Year of Decision*. In both he had tried to say something previously unsaid about his native West and its relation to the nation as a whole.

DeVoto also understood that he was writing his great history backward. Garrett Mattingly joked that he suffered from a severe case of "regressus historicus"—the irrepressible urge to search endlessly for "the background of the background of the background." Mattingly's diagnosis was correct: in his friend's immediate future lay an annotated edition of the journals of Lewis and Clark and a massive account of the clash of three European empires in the New World beginning in the sixteenth century. DeVoto was forced to admit that his original interest had centered on the Civil War, and in fact he had taken the revisionist school of Civil War historians to task for their argument that the war had been a "repressible conflict." But with his nagging concern with beginnings he had turned to the moment when his region had emerged to play a defining role in the national drama. Now he had discovered an earlier transitional point when a thousand or so fur trappers managed to finish themselves off as makers of the country's future. DeVoto caught the moment of "splendid transit of past and future" in August 1839, when Joe Meek, one of the last of the trappers, meets the first wagon train headed toward Oregon.

> Joe Meek, the bear killer, a Carson man, a Bridger man, a Company man—Joe Meek, free trapper, raised his hand and rode off toward Fort Davy Crockett. And the other three greenhorns, authentic settlers, and their Snake guide took the trail again, toward the Columbia.

As Wallace Stegner, who took the whole intermountain West as his backyard, pointed out later, the forty-nine-year-old DeVoto had never toured his native region in any depth and had written his two volumes "as an avid and intuitive reader of maps." Now, in 1946, as he prepared to edit the journals of Lewis and Clark, DeVoto realized the need for a close inspection and embarked with his family on a lengthy pilgrimage. On June 1, the DeVotos headed west and for three months wandered the region from Colorado's Rocky

Mountain National Park, where he consulted Park Service personnel, to the Canadian border, from Glacier and Yellowstone to Devil's Gate and Independence Rock, and even Ogden, "the scurvy little Mormon Catholic dump that created all my neuroses." All along the route he stopped to talk with the Park Service and Forest Service people, rangers as well as regional directors like Struthers Burt of Jackson Hole and Chet Olsen of the Dude Ranchers Association, already firm epistolary friends. By the time he returned to Cambridge in September he had acquired an entire network of correspondents and informants on the activities of the cattlemen and their plans for a landgrab. There were the writers A.B. Guthrie and Stewart Holbrook in Oregon, Joseph Kinsey Howard in Montana, Struthers Burt in Wyoming, the indispensable Arthur Carhart in Denver, and Frank Dobie in Austin. These together with local members of the Wilderness Society and the Isaak Walton League continued to feed him reports on the doings of the stockmen.

It was Chet Olsen in the regional office of the Forest Service in Ogden who handed DeVoto a list of the resolutions adopted by a joint meeting of the American Livestock Association and the National Woolgrowers Association demanding the return of federal lands to the states for redistribution to themselves. In apprising DeVoto of the projected landgrab, Olsen, according to Stegner, handed him "the cause and controversy that took precedence over all other causes and controversies of his contentious career, the one that most enlisted his heart, conscience and knowledge." DeVoto, he concluded, had headed west in 1946 as a tourist and historian and returned as a devout conservationist and dangerous adversary.

In fact, DeVoto had been hammering home the facts of ongoing exploitation in the West for a dozen years, ever since his "The Plundered Province" article appeared in *Harper's* in August 1934.

Now, however, his focus had shifted from a concentration on Eastern financial interests to the homegrown despoilers pursuing their own policies of exploitation. Primed and loaded by his Western contingent of observers, DeVoto returned to Cambridge and quickly opened fire on the grazing interests in two *Harper's* essays in December 1946 and January 1947. In his opening salvo, "The Anxious West," he set his sights on the American celebration of the myth of the cowboy West propagated by Hollywood—the image of the fearless, unsmiling dispenser of justice. Such ceremonials were not without their unintended irony, he commented, for no other Western business interest—not even the nefarious Amalgamated Copper—was less regardful of the public interest and people's rights. None were more destructive, none more exploitative.

But it was the follow-up piece that sharpened his indictment of Western waste and despoliation and applied it to those little people who in their refusal to realize that in countenancing and even defending the large predators they were helping to liquidate their own resources. Westerners, he scoffed, had bought into the scam, joining in the looting under the cover of a ridiculous mythology that bore no relation to the fact of increasing degradation. The process of looting the land, DeVoto knew now, had begun with those mountain men who wiped out the beaver all the while trumpeting their freedom from an overcivilized East and the capitalist monopoly that was exploiting them. Next in the parade of plunderers would come the cattlemen and the sheepmen followed by mining syndicates and the timber industry—all of them fighting federal regulation and issuing their demand to "get out and send more money." Ranged against these selfish interests throughout the history of the West were the legitimate stewards of the land, those permanent settlers whose story he had told in *The Year of Decision*, families like his Grandfather Dye's, scrabbling for a living and laboriously building up the country. "They made farms and set up local systems of production, trade, export of surpluses, and even manufacture." They were, in short, Populism's little people whose descendants now stood in dire need of information and education. Then he would supply it. Both Wests—the giant grazing interests and the small outfits alike—were pursuing a fantasy of unlimited resources and chasing the dream of a quick buck. Left to their own devices they would soon make their industries an impossibility. "That," DeVoto added in sounding a new prophetic note, "is not the greatest danger. For if the watersheds go, and they will go if cattlemen and sheepmen are allowed to get rid of government regulations of grazing, the West will go too—farms, ranches, towns, cities, irrigation systems, power plants, business in general." Then came the clincher: "The United States cannot afford to let this happen. You cannot afford to." By 1948 DeVoto was busy fighting the stockmen and their intended landgrab on several fronts. He was searching Congress for recruits and placing articles—his own and others'—wherever he could and extending his editorial reach into the popular magazines. He was also seeking connections in the West among the opponents of the grazing interests, able writers and spokesmen for land conservation. He sent urgent requests to Struthers Burt for names of the conspirators plotting to get their hands on the public domain. "Tell me everybody you think is in it, all the big bastards, all the little sons of bitches." Above all, send facts! "R'ar back and let fly at me."

This was his marching order to Wallace Stegner, who had been keeping track of his friend's activities from Stanford. When Stegner wrote to him expressing admiration for his exposure of the attempted landgrab, DeVoto sent back his instructions. "If you feel like that, goddamit, get into print with it—we need everybody in print we can get." Stegner required little coaxing. His urge to do something in behalf of his beliefs had grown stronger ever since his study of Clarence Dutton ten years earlier. Now having just finished his evocative folk history of his home country, he was examining the career of Dutton's boss, John Wesley Powell. He was fully prepared to enlist.

II

In their years together in Cambridge during World War II Wallace Stegner and Bernard DeVoto became fast friends and supportive colleagues. Following a hectic editorial interval in New York, DeVoto had returned to relative contentment if not peace and quiet in his home near the university, and Stegner and Mary with their young son, Page, moved from suburban Newtonville to Cambridge's Trowbridge Street within walking distance of his friend's house. Wally and Mary and Benny and Avis, as they came to call each other, soon became close acquaintances and frequent guests, with the Stegners reliable participants in the DeVotos' bibulous Sunday Evening Hours, which lasted well into the night and ended with one of Avis's improvised suppers. The two men played badminton and tennis together, Benny in his jerky swat-'em style, Wally with a grace honed by long practice. Both men indulged in advertising their Western credentials, DeVoto with his patented tough-guy irreverence, Stegner, his voice mellowed by his host's libations, by occasionally breaking into a rendition of "The Cowboy's Lament." Stegner's circle of friends quickly broadened to include most of the younger members of Harvard's English department as well as outside colleagues including the social psychologist Gordon Allport. Harvard provided cultural riches and intellectual stimuli new to the Stegners, but it also demanded a full quota of teaching composition, an exacting job at which Stegner and his teaching assistant, Mark Schorer, excelled. It was at this time, too, that he befriended Robert Frost, whose poetry he admired inordinately and whose crusty Yankee manner intrigued him.

Stegner taught hard and well, returning to his own vast array of projects late at night or early in the morning. These were various: an outsized manuscript planned as a trilogy but defying completion as *The Big Rock Candy Mountain*; another unsuccessful novel, *Fire and Ice*, based on his observations of the activities of the Young Communist League at the University of Wisconsin a few years earlier; and several of his best short stories drawn from events in his childhood—"The Colt," "Butcher Bird," "Goin' to Town," and "Two Rivers." His jam-packed schedule, which rivaled DeVoto's, included advice in print to would-be authors on the importance of form in crafting fiction, advice he himself was already applying in writing history. Form, he agreed with DeVoto, was "the most difficult and at the same time the most essential problem of writing." As his new friend Robert Frost explained, "It takes imagination to put form on experience," a trick Stegner was beginning to master.

All of Stegner's forms rested on that middle ground between fiction and history that he constantly traversed. "I defend the middle ground as one who has strayed there several times," he admitted. Despite the intensive research into the Wobbly's life and times, he defined his story of the Industrial Workers of the World martyr Joe Hill as a novel: a fictional arrangement of invented characters and scenes and dialogue "bent," as he put it, to his artistic purposes. *Beyond the Hundredth Meridian*, his portrait of John Wesley Powell, on the contrary, was biography pure and simple although here too, he confessed, he could be caught "warping" certain abstractions and "ideal" proportions. His intention in both his fiction and his history, he explained, was "clearly novelistic in its emphasis on human interest, but historical in that I wanted to be faithful to fact and record." It was this "visceral history" he sought as his chosen form.

Stegner's middle ground stance between fact and fiction pleased neither the historians who were insistent on keeping the two realms separate nor the literary critics who disapproved of his excessive reliance on personal experiences and memories as his warping tool. But Stegner, like DeVoto, also had a quarrel with the professionals and academicians who dismissed popular history written as story as "something faintly disreputable, the proper playground of lady novelists." Good history could be assembled from documents, policy statements, memoranda, and position papers, he agreed, but great history is stories that grip the reader.

In 1940 George Stegner committed suicide in Salt Lake City after killing the woman with whom he was living, a last act of destruction which left his son with a mixture of anger, resentment, shame, and sadness with which he would not come to terms until four decades later in *Recapitulation* (1979), a long-postponed sequel to *The Big Rock Candy Mountain*. It was not the death of his father but a professional and personal need to return home that determined Wallace and Mary to abandon temporarily their summer farmhouse in Vermont for a trip to Utah and the Plateau Province—what he would call "Mormon Country" in his next book and his first piece of genuine history. Just as DeVoto headed west in 1940 to sharpen his sense of direction as he prepared to finish *The Year of Decision*, so a year later Wallace Stegner came home to the Mountain West to reacquaint himself with the sites of his childhood before undertaking his folk history. At the urging of his new publisher, Duell, Sloan and Pearce, he had agreed to contribute a volume on the intermountain region to the company's American Folkways Series. Out of the trip west and ongoing consultations with Utah friends and Mormon historians came the book in 1942, Stegner's first excursion into popular history. *Mormon Country* is folk history with a difference, for it provides a key to the author's emerging politics and social philosophy which, like DeVoto's, pointed him toward a democratic populism and the nurturing of a civic conscience in the country's producing classes.

At first glance *Mormon Country* seems a loose collection of profiles and vignettes, anecdotes and legends dotting the historical landscape from Brigham Young's dictatorial reign to the day-before-yesterday in the Plateau Province. In addition to a portrait of Brigham Young there is a brief sketch of John Wesley Powell, whose career Stegner was beginning to examine in detail. Although authority rules in Salt Lake City, the center of Mormon Country, it does not rule the strange doings of schismatics and eccentrics out in the barren provinces. All along Stegner's route through Mormon Country readers encounter heroes and villains, visionaries and reactionaries, exhorters and backsliders with the author serving as guide and commentator, spicing his stories with personal opinions and scattering them throughout his account with an even hand.

Interest in Stegner's popular history, among Mormons and Gentiles alike, centered on the author's judgment of the Church. The faithful dismissed the book as a product of misinformation and bias while critics of the Mormons like DeVoto considered it much too generous. The truth, like the meaning of Stegner's politics, lay somewhere in between in memories of his adolescent years in Salt Lake City and the welcome accorded a shy and awkward newcomer at the Church's Ward House. As a boy Stegner spent nearly a decade in the flourishing city, happily accepting the Mormons' welcoming ways. Yet no more than DeVoto, whose earlier contacts with the Church in Ogden had been so confrontational, could Stegner, then or later, take Mormon theology seriously. And like his friend he remained highly critical of the authoritarian structure of the Church hierarchy, and strongly disapproving of the closed minds of its true believers. Nevertheless, he clearly recalled the general good will fostered by Mormonism and the family solidarity he had never experienced before. The lonely and diffident youngster off the prairies had wanted more than anything to "belong to something." As he recalled, "I suppose one of the things that made me feel friendly to the Mormons all my life is the fact that, in Utah, again a waif and torn again from any kind of association and friendship, somebody took me down to the Ward House one Tuesday night and here was all this going on and everybody belonging to something."

These warm memories were cooled by a disapproval of the dictatorial ways of the Church itself, its practice of censorship, its bizarre theology, and the smugness of too many of its practitioners. To outsiders, he explained, Mormonism seemed the "product of the ignorance and witchcraft of the frontier, the pseudo-science of amateur anthropologists and sociologists, the ignorance and superstition of the underprivileged people of Europe who became converts." Such blanket condemnation by the outside world Stegner knew to be rude and unjust, but he also realized that a rigid fundamentalism rich in miracles, revelations, prophecies, and myriad gifts of the spirit was the breeding ground for a fanaticism among believers that would brook no opposition. Power lodged in a patriarchy that held benighted views of blacks and women necessarily provided "its share of bigots, parochial intolerants, and authoritarians." The top-heavy structure of church and family ensured inequity: "The Church has fostered rigidity of belief, even a brand of theocratic statism, has consistently kept women in their place as cooks, housekeepers, and breeding machines, and has subjugated the individual small-fry Mormon to the authority of the priesthood." Bernard DeVoto could scarcely have improved on this indictment.

Yet it was just those small-fry Mormons down in the arid Plateau Province in the southern parts of the state who presented the more appealing side of the Mormon faith—grit, determination, endurance, neighborly concern, and instinctive cooperation—people much like Bernard DeVoto's grandfather, Samuel Dye. Two quite different characters embodied these qualities for Stegner albeit in opposite ways: J. Golden Kimball, the Will Rogers of Mormonism, exhorter and keeper of the flame, who combined the faith of the zealot with the salty talk of the frontiersman; and Jesse Knight, paternalist entrepreneur and builder of smokeless, drinkless, and whoreless mining towns for his employees, putting his money where it would do the most good. Both of these Mormon impulses—to exhortation and philanthropy—had been seriously weakened by 1940 although they still survived along that north-south axis of broad plateaus studded with buttes and mesas, "the land nobody wanted." Here in a country the Gentiles wouldn't settle, it is just possible for the faithful to eke out a living, if not by farming the arid region then by stock-raising.

In the twentieth century, however, the crop most Mormons tend is history. "Take it as a general rule all over Mormon Country that people who started out a hundred years ago to build the future have built instead a past. . . . The rock the fathers planted was the future; the crop the sons harvest is the past." No one, not even the faithful, believes in a future utopia. "Mammon has won most of the battles, the peculiar social organization of Mormonism has grown more like that of the world outside."

At this point in his story Stegner, his verdict rendered, shifts attention to the Gentiles of Mormon Country, the Saints' former enemies and rivals and present collaborators in economic development. In the second section of the book, which he entitled "The Might of the Gentiles," he explains how Mormonism has become less and less a religion apart as the Gentile exploitation of the region's resources proceeds apace. Rapidly disappearing or already gone are many of the prophetic elements of Mormonism and with them the original idea of a planned economy. One of the "curious facts" he notes is the decline of hopes for a managed economy among the Saints at the very moment when these hopes have become stronger throughout the rest of the world. "Mormonism reveals itself as an economic empire, an empire of dollars instead of the dreamed empire of men. By the time the world knows enough to learn from Mormonism and other societies with a similar sense of dedication to an ideal, Mormonism has been converted to the other side." Mormons and Gentiles have now pooled their resources and combined their moneymaking talents in the shared manipulation of dollars. With the discovery of vast sources of copper came the cyanide mills and corporate consolidation and John D. Rockefeller's arrival. "Railroads, smelters, concentration plants, flotation plants, all the apparatus of large-scale mining went in, and the profits boomed. Co-operation continued." With monopoly capitalism came union-busting and contempt for the Greek, Italian, Serb, Mexican, and Japanese miners who provided the profits and lived in poverty. "Let 'em alone as long as they come to work," became the corporate watchword.

Accommodation and ongoing exploitation of people and the land mean that whatever hope remains rests with Stegner's heroes—those independent, nonpolitical seekers after a different truth, explorers and investigators who reject power and possessions for larger social goals, civic aims, and scientific truth. There is a line of succession in *Mormon Country* from the pathfinder and explorer Jed Smith, who, unlike his Mountain Men companions, is content to study the country and find new routes across it. And in a later day the geologist-anthropologist Earl Douglass satisfied with unearthing the bones of Tertiary mammals along the Plateau canyons, "a Heaven-hunter of a different breed." And the greatest of them all, Stegner was beginning to realize, was John Wesley Powell, explorer, scientist, planner, and institution builder with his own dream for the West. Here were the genuine heroes of the intermountain region—disinterested seekers, free from aggrandizement and dedicated to advancing knowledge for the benefit of all the people. The line of progression from *Mormon Country* in 1942 to *Beyond the Hundredth Meridian* twelve years later was direct.

Stegner's celebration of the hero affords a clue to his politics, which is best described as middle-of-the-road liberalism. Like DeVoto he feared unchecked power and arbitrary authority, which he knew were fed by dogma and ideological abstractions. Both men called for "facts," by which they meant empiricism and deductive logic. But Stegner in particular dreaded fanaticism as the breeder of hatred. Hatred, he insisted, divided the self into warring halves of ends and means and led directly to totalitarian abuse. He first addressed this problem in an exploratory political novel, *Fire and Ice* (1941), which probed the moral disintegration of a young Communist whose hatred becomes all-consuming. The novel was another of the author's admitted failures because it is dominated by a stark syllogism: abstractions lead to unchecked power; unchecked power feeds on hatred; hatred ends in moral irresponsibility and ultimately inhumanity. Stegner's antihero, poor boy and student leader of the Young Communist League at a Midwestern university, grows increasingly resentful, suspicious, conspiratorial, and brutal until, following an attempted assault of a sorority coed, he sees the light, repents, and leaves college in order to find himself. If the novel is flawed (and Stegner cheerfully admitted its shortcomings), the author's distrust of ideology, whether left or right, is clear: unchecked anger leads to political hatred and ends in abuse of power. Stegner would dramatize this argument with greater success some years later in *The Preacher and the Slave*, later retitled *Joe Hill*.

Bernard DeVoto's reaction to the Second World War helped send him back to a mid-nineteenth-century Great West as the source of a vital democratic nationalism and a distinct American identity. Wallace Stegner's response to the war impelled him in another direction in a search for an alternative definition of nationalism, one that was culturally decentered and racially and ethnically multiple. Part of this new sense of diversity stemmed from his wartime teaching at Harvard, which had introduced courses for the Army's Specialized Training Program. Here he encountered bright young draftees from all regions and classes, "eager guys," he commented, "wide-eyed and lapping it up and loving it," yet on campus for a single semester only before being shipped out "to lose the top of their heads." Teaching such a wide variety of young men in wartime, Stegner found an exacting and even perilous task. Wars, he agreed with DeVoto, tend to clamp down on the expression of ideas and the examination of values as the results of fascism in Germany and Italy so clearly proved. Somehow Americans would have to avoid such conformism and repression.

Thus when the editors of *Look* magazine approached him in 1944 with a suggestion that he, together with its photographers, travel the country to see how the nation's minorities were faring, he jumped at the chance, taking a leave from Harvard in order to undertake the assignment. Stegner welcomed this assignment in investigative photojournalism, as he explained, in order to swap the "monastic distance of the campus" for hit-the-road adventure. He was not entirely sure that he wanted to stay at Harvard even if given tenure. Moreover, he was an inveterate traveler, living proof, he would admit, that true Westerners were "born on wheels." All his life he combined love of familiarity and permanence with an urge to discover new peoples and places. DeVoto, given a goodly supply of books, manuscripts, and maps, could write his history in the confines of his Berkeley Street study with only an occasional jaunt westward. Stegner enjoyed no such imaginative luxury: he had to see for himself. Now in the summer of 1944 he made forays into rural North Carolina and Southside Chicago to report on conditions for blacks in both settings. Then, following another stint at Bread Loaf, he headed west with Mary and Page, stopping in at Santa Fe, where he met Ansel Adams and began a lifelong friendship, before moving on to Santa Barbara and setting up a home base for his investigative work. The result was not the original projected series of magazine articles on the topic of prejudice, which the editors suddenly deemed too controversial, but a survey separately published and entitled *One Nation* which appeared just as the war ended.

One Nation, which combined Stegner's evenhanded assessments and *Look*'s camera work, struck readers as a vivid piece of investigative photojournalism. The narrative and photographs documented a wide variety of minority places and peoples—from Filipinos in West Coast cities to Boston's Irish Catholic community. In collecting his impressions Stegner indulged his passion for travel as an essential preliminary to actual reportage as he scouted the country in successive trips and excursions. He traveled to Santa Fe for interviews with Hispanics and tours of the pueblos; to Southside Chicago and small-town North Carolina for a first-hand view of black life in the South and urban ghettos; to war relocation camps for Japanese-Americans and pachuco neighbor-hoods in Los Angeles—exploring new locales and their peoples.

Stegner's opening chapter, entitled "The Unaccepted," states the argument that runs through the entire report. "There is a wall down the middle of America, a wall of suspicion, distrust, snob-bery, hatred, and guilt." On one side of the wall live so-called WASPS; on the other, people who because of race, color, religion, or ethnicity are denied full American citizenship. The problem, his investigations had convinced him, was a national one. "We do not have, specifically, and separately, a Jewish problem, a Catholic problem, a Mexican or Oriental problem. We have one national problem." The postwar American challenge as it appears in all of the minority profiles is how to maintain unity in diversity, how to join together different peoples into a loose but comprehensive federation without forced conformity or sacrifice of distinct cul-tures. Though the phrase had yet to be invented, Stegner was calling for a vital American cultural pluralism.

Texts and photographs complement each other effectively. In the report on Filipinos in Los Angeles, for example, on the left page appears President Roosevelt's promise of Philippine independence followed by Stegner's remark that "There is no doubt how we feel about the Philippines." On the facing page is a stark shot of a flop-house entrance with a faded sign announcing rooms to be had for 50¢–75¢ but competing with a bright white-on-black message on the door reading "POSITIVELY NO FILIPINOS ALLOWED." Beneath the photograph stands Stegner's terse question: "How about our feeling toward Filipinos?" The chapter on relocated Japanese-

Americans is equally hard-hitting with pictures of the evacuees coping with every kind of deprivation with their own doctors and nurses, teachers and schools. Interspersed are Stegner's comments and quiet condemnation of the centers as "neither prisons, concentration camps, reservations, nor refuges" but with "qualities of each." Blame for the enormity lies not simply with a benighted military but with civilian prejudice, "a synthetic product, constantly fomented by such organizations as the Native Sons of the Golden West, the Home Front Commandos, and some American Legion and Veterans of Foreign War posts, and stirred vigorously by the Hearst press."

The course followed by these successive reports runs from west to east, from war relocation centers, Chinatowns in San Francisco and Los Angeles, migrant Mexican worker camps in the state's Central Valley to Hispanic villages and Native American pueblos in the Southwest then on to blacks in a Jim Crow South and ghettoized Chicago and finally to Jews in New York and Boston's Irish fending off anti-Catholic bigotry while tolerating anti-Semitism in their neighborhoods. In fact, Stegner earlier had written a highly critical piece on Father Coughlin, calling attention to the radio priest's virulent anti-Semitism, and between 1944 and 1946 had published a number of articles in the popular magazines on prejudice and bigotry as constituting the most serious challenge to postwar American democracy.

Stegner's analysis becomes more objective, even clinical, as he moves eastward from the West Coast to less familiar urban sites and situations. Black Americans, while grievously discriminated against in both North and South, appeared to him to possess fewer resources familial or educational for throwing off the dysfunctional effects of slavery. While agreeing with Lillian Smith that "the real Negro problem is the white man," Stegner saw only marginal improvement for a recent black arrival in Northern cities. Though he enjoys better schooling and a wider access to civic culture, "by comparison with the white American he is still a second-class citizen."

Stegner reserved his deepest understanding and sympathy for those minorities in the Arid Regions—Hispanic Americans and Native Americans eking out a living from the stingy soil. Hispanic Americans, he assured readers, possessed "a pretty wonderful community sense, a knack for working together that living in a barren country taught them." Theirs was a simple, even primitive agriculture, family-based, craft-oriented, tradition-driven, "a culture strange to other Americans, Spanish in all its ways, primitive and unmechanized, unfitted to cope on equal terms with the competitive society which swallowed it." Hispanic-American society in some ways resembled rural Vermont, static, adapted, and "rooted in three hundred years of permanence." But in those three centuries the minority peoples of the Southwest together with the land they worked had grown steadily poorer. Once under the old Spanish system landless men scratched out a living as stock raisers on the *ejidos*, communally owned pastures and open range, but the *ejidos* are gone now, taxed out of existence and bought up by the big stockmen with their commercial herds, which have stripped the grass and ruined the land. "Result: a wasteful run-off of lifegiving water, floods with every rain and every spring thaw, a steady pouring of the best topsoil into the Rio Grande." Hispanic poverty, though not marked by the social disintegration that strikes poor people in less stable cultures, nevertheless cuts deep, and children go shoeless and hungry. In a photograph of two youngsters, one with shoes full of holes, the other barefoot, Stegner's collaborating photographer made a visual condemnation reminiscent of Jacob Riis in *How the Other Half Lives*.

Stegner found similar forms of communal cooperation among Native Americans, the "least known Americans," he called them, on whom a policy of forced Americanization had levied a prohibitive toll, pauperizing and demoralizing tribes penned up on reservations with "too little good land, too little water." Yet various Indian tribes, like the Hispanic Americans on their lands, retained "the Indian habit of working together" now strengthened by actions of the federal government. "Co-operative enterprises have sprung up, run by Indians for Indians: grocery stores, cattle herds, sawmills, dairies." All partial but hopeful signs, especially since Washington was presently lending a hand with the Forest Service, the Soil Conservation Service, and other federal agencies cooperating with local peoples in reviving inherited cooperative cultures.

As the war ended, both Wallace and Mary Stegner looked to cooperatives as opening a middle way between a predatory corporate capitalism and a repressive collectivism. She was an active socialist, he a strong sympathizer with his wife's principles yet loath to relinquish valuable writing time for prosletyzing, which he left to her. The outcome of the war nevertheless strengthened both their hopes for cooperatives, a brief history of which he had published in a series of articles in 1942 and 1943. When Stegner arrived at Stanford in June 1945 to take up his teaching duties, he and Mary joined a recently formed housing cooperative, the Peninsula Housing Association, in an attempt to create a communally managed neighborhood. The cooperative collapsed when its four hundred members failed to secure FHA loans. Wallace and Mary left the failing cooperative and bought a hilltop property in Los Altos with a striking view of the surrounding hills. Stegner did much of the finishing work on the low-slung house, as he had with the Vermont farmhouse, priding himself on laying a long brick terrace and embracing a large live oak with surrounding deck.

Despite the setback to their hopes for communal cooperatives both Stegners held fast to their strong faith in local associations as an alternative to statism and unchecked individualism—a sensible working partnership between government and its citizens on the ground. This partnership had been the dream of John Wesley Powell, the great nineteenth-century explorer, land planner, scientist, and institution builder whose life and achievements Stegner had studied for some time.

Page Stegner recalls traveling with his father as a young boy of eight or nine on Wallace's seemingly endless wanderings across his home country in preparation for writing about Powell. "My father . . . could never just *look* at scenery. If we happened to be driving across the Colorado Plateau through southern Utah, say from Cisco to Price along the Book Cliffs, he'd offer up an anecdote about Powell being rescued by Bradley in Desolation Canyon, and then explain to his slightly annoyed eight-year-old boy (me), who was trying to concentrate on his Batman comic, who Powell was and why he was important." The land held history in its grip, Stegner was convinced, and the meaning of both could be discovered only by the making of paths across it, as he would put it in *Wolf Willow*. "He had a kind of holistic relationship with the land," his son recalled, "and he couldn't look at it without remembering its geological history, its exploration, its social development, its contemporary problems, and its prognosis for the future." Stegner always needed to know exactly where he stood, and that meant noting contour, climate, color, look, and smell. This acute sense of place would be keenest in the opening section of his biography of John Wesley Powell, finally completed after years of work in 1953 and published a year later. But it was also evident in his 1950 novel *The Preacher and the Slave* (reissued as *Joe Hill*) with its evocations of the Seattle-Tacoma waterfront,

California Central Valley hopfields, and a provincial Salt Lake City early in the twentieth century.

Joe Hill, another of Stegner's commercial failures, is significant in two respects. First, as a clear political statement by the author. And second, as marking a turning away from fiction to the completion of his major piece of historical writing. Stegner's interest in the life and legend of the martyr Joe Hill of the Industrial Workers of the World labor union was a long-standing one. A school friend in Salt Lake City had been a member of the family of the owner of the meat market next door to the grocery store where Joe Hill allegedly killed the grocer and his son. "I used to take out the daughter of the warden of the State Pen when I was a freshman in college or maybe a senior in high school so that I knew the old State Pen on Twenty-first South pretty well," he told an interviewer years later. While researching the story of Joe Hill he prevailed upon the new warden of the penitentiary to walk him through a mock execution—from Joe Hill's cell, down the iron stairs, across the yard and up the alley, "stopping in front of a door with a canvas screen across it, the execution gear tossed into an old shed, complete with broken armchair they strapped Joe Hill to, and the steel-plated backstop." All this, he explained, to get a "criminal's eye-view" of what it felt like to be walked out to your death.

Before finishing his novel Stegner published two essays on Joe Hill, one in an academic journal depicting the organizer as an "ambiguous bindle stiff" transformed by the IWW into a martyr; the second, "Joe Hill: The Wobblies Troubador," which appeared in the *New Republic* and touched off protests and picketing by remnants of the One Big Union. Both articles presented Joe Hill in an unfavorable light as a "stick-up" man more violent and fanatical than his comrades. The Joe Hill of the novel, however, is a more complicated and sympathetic character, a moody aspiring artist, "a player of the piano at local meetings, a maker of catchy rhymes and drawer of cartoons" who was known to leave behind a sketch on the back of a laundry ticket or the lyrics to a new song. Yet always a loner, "a man with a hot temper and no really close friends," and "a rebel from his skin inwards." In short, a man driven to extremes in whom a revolutionary urge warred with an aesthetic need and who knew all along "how everything he did was not enough."

Stegner reponded somewhat lamely to sharp criticism from the left and dismissals by the Cold War right, insisting that his book was neither history nor biography, but fiction "with fiction's prerogatives and none of history's limiting obligations." He had sought a different truth attainable only after myths and legends had been dispelled. A less equivocal reply restated his political beliefs. "I have been convinced for a long time that what is miscalled the middle of the road is actually the most radical and the most difficult position—much more difficult and radical than either reaction or rebellion."

Rebellion too often doesn't distinguish sufficiently, and it commonly rebels against too much. To get rid of Rockefeller or Weyerhaeuser . . . it often burns Plato, Aristotle, and Hull House. And reaction has nothing to do but cling—all life becomes a hanging-on, a clutching. Neither extreme has to think, to sort out, to make discriminations, judgments, to act rationally. All it has to do is to throb, and sometimes it throbs with admirable courage. I guess I would agree . . . about the goodness of the Wobbly heart and the weakness of the Wobbly head. I guess I am going to interpret Joe Hill as a man rebelling too far.

Such sentiments appeared to echo a Cold War call for a vital American center, but in a deeper sense they were the long-held convictions of a nonpolitical advocate of literary realism, scientific method, and civic virtue—of an approach to life, that is, like that of John Wesley Powell, whose illustrious career seemed to Stegner a model of citizenship.

Stegner was bitterly disappointed by the reception accorded *Joe Hill*. He later recalled his mood in an interview: "I thought, 'Oh, Christ, I'm throwing pearls before swine and sounding off in the wilderness where there are no receivers tuned in.'" Suddenly his limitations as a novelist seemed palpable, and he decided to quit writing fiction, at least for a while, because he seemed to be on the wrong track. "I frankly thought I was a kind of anachronism. I thought I was a nineteenth-century prairie child trying to write for the twentieth century—and it wouldn't work."

In a more profound sense than he realized as he turned from exploding myths to hunting for a hero, Stegner, like his friend Bernard DeVoto, *was* a stepchild of a postfrontier nineteenth century. Powell's appeal to him was of long standing. Civil War hero, pathbreaking explorer, scientific innovator, and institution builder, Powell loomed large in the environmental imagination as offering a needed corrective to the mindless development and exploitation that characterized the mid-twentieth century. It was Powell, along with his lieutenant Clarence Dutton, who had first taught Stegner the harsh truths of the Arid Region. Powell's definition of the Arid Region as a dry core of eight public-land states—Arizona, Colorado, Idaho, Montana, Nevada, New Mexico, Utah, and Wyoming—coincided with Stegner's remembered world of what Powell was the first to call the Plateau Province. Powell's heroic Colorado River exploit, moreover, was barely two generations removed from Stegner's boyhood years in the slickrock country.

Most important, Stegner insisted, were the lessons Powell taught concerning the limits nature had placed on the settlement and development of the arid West. "Not the Pacific Coast furiously bent on becoming Conurbia from Portland to San Diego. Forget the metropolitan sprawl of Denver, Phoenix, Tucson, Albuquerque, Dallas–Fort Worth and Salt Lake City, growing to the limits of their water and beyond, like bacterial cultures overflowing the edges of their agar dishes and beginning to sicken on their own wastes." The real West—his own West—lay beyond the 100th meridian where rainfall averaged less than sixteen to twenty inches annually, that rising dry country DeVoto's emigrants had crossed on their way to Oregon and California. Here was Major Powell's country as well.

Completing the portrait of John Wesley Powell on which he had been working off and on for nearly a decade confronted Stegner with the problem he always identified for his students—the problem of form. His study of Powell, he realized, was not to be a standard biography, for he cared little about the major's private life. Nor was it, strictly speaking, history as the academicians wrote it, suitably objective and distanced. Like DeVoto he was determined to enter his story in his own person as guide, interpreter, and critic as the situation demanded. At first the challenge of form seemed daunting, and he was puzzled and disheartened, as he confessed to DeVoto. "I am really scared to death to let anybody see this, for some reason." He was afraid that he was faltering because he was not sure of his intended readers, whether "the great unwashed" or "the twelve experts on Colorado River explorations." It was not merely a matter of style or voice, he told Benny, but the need to make the form of his story carry the meaning, and he was not sure that he was up to the task.

DeVoto recognized his friend's problem as a familiar one and hastened to the rescue. Stegner was suffering from a severe attack of the "literary megrims," the lingering effect of "a previously undramatized part of your adolescence." "Why, you God-damned idiot, this is a distinguished book. For Christ's sweet sake! Stop beating your breast and earn some writer's cramp." From back-handed compliments DeVoto turned to specifics and useful advice. Yes, Stegner did need those first two chapters as a verbal map and an account of heroic adventure down the Colorado River. No, his chapters were not too long, for they were essential in all their detail for the ensuing story of scientific exploration, planning, and institutional leadership. More might be made of Henry Adams, he told Stegner, the prophet of gloom and doom who, like the Eastern *literati*, turned his back on the West and thus provided the measure of Major Powell's achievements. Then DeVoto addressed one of his friend's persistent worries—a fear of losing narrative momentum when he stopped to summarize and analyze Powell's ideas. DeVoto would have none of it. "Don't you tell those privileged to listen to you in class that there are various forms of narrative and that narrative effects are secured by various means?" DeVoto's advice grew more specific and insistent as he read on, but first he half-apologized for marking up the manuscript without permission. "None of my damned business to tell you how to write or what to do," but he proceeded to make valuable suggestions for improvement. When Stegner approached a climax in his story, he should make it a climax. And help the reader out "by locating him in space and on the map wherever you can, which is oftener than you do by a good deal." And above all, keep your chronology straight—a challenge he himself was presently confronting in compiling his massive account of the exploration and settlement of the New World, *The Course of Empire*. Keep tossing dates at the reader.

You've got to keep saying, Now this is happening in 1492, in fact on October 12, and what I am talking about in this aside happened in 1641, in a premature snowstorm; and Joe Doakes was the guy who pushed a peanut up Pike's Peak, that was in 1702 and he was lefthanded and beat his wife. Keep saying, Pissant Pass is due west of Concord, Middlesex County, Massachusetts, about six miles, take Highway 2 or the new bypass. Or, right now he's where the Union Pacific crosses Highway 30 four miles outside of Paradise Junction, there used to be a whorehouse there but now there's only a Socony station.

End of advice! "But Jesus! you're screwy. This is a swell book, and there's nothing wrong with it, you've handled it marvelously well, you will continue to. Get in there and pitch. Any questions?"

Stegner paid tribute to DeVoto by dedicating the Powell book to him "in gratitude for a hundred kindnesses, the latest of which is the present introduction, but the earliest of which goes back nearly twenty years." DeVoto reciprocated with an appreciative introduction which, however, by way of a corrective skewered academic historians for their neglect of Powell. Not the most effective way to promote a friend's book even though DeVoto's claim for its importance as *national* history—"inseparable from the central energies of American history"—was right on the mark.

Stegner met DeVoto's challenge and adopted his friend's time-tested method in his opening account of Powell's career by introducing one of the major's many adversaries, this one the blue-sky booster and master of geopolitical bombast, the Honorable William Gilpin. Aging Jacksonian frontiersman, Indian fighter, Civil War veteran, and in 1869, governor of the Colorado Territory, Gilpin was a voluble prophet of unlimited western expansion. It was Gilpin who propagated the fantasy of a High Plains Paradise—no forests to be cleared, ample water from artesian wells, neither extreme heat nor numbing cold, no droughts or cloudbursts—nothing, in short, to hinder the foreordained spread of continental empire to Pacific shores. Though he could scarcely envision the enormity of his educational task as he set out on his expedition down the Colorado, John Wesley Powell would have his work cut out for him in disabusing the American public of the nonsense propagated by William Gilpin and his tribe.

Gilpin was only the first and least threatening of Major Powell's rivals and enemies in a list that lengthened annually throughout his thirty-year career in the service of science and democracy. There was, for another example, one Sam Adams—no kin to Henry but a spiritual sibling of DeVoto's Lansford Hastings—who manufactured tales of discovery and derring-do that were travesties of reality. Braggart, imposter, mountebank, evil genius, Sam Adams would dog the major's footsteps across the West and into Washington, D.C., with his claims of explorations never conducted and facts never verified. A constant presence, Adams, according to Stegner, hovered just beyond "the shadow line which divides the merely extravagant from the lunatic."

Henry Adams, friend and sponsor of Powell's rival scientific explorer, Clarence King, remains a distant negative presence in Stegner's telling, a different scientific synthesizer interpreting American history with the aid of the second law of thermodynamics as an accelerating slide toward a final state of entropy. Adams's pessimism makes a perfect foil for Major Powell's faith in government-sponsored scientific planning. Clarence King, Henry Adams's friend and protégé, a brilliant scientist and surveyor of the West, is the superior of Powell in education and expertise but lacks the major's powers of concentration and endurance and prefers wealth to intellectual acclaim. King eventually abandons governmental science for a futile search for a mining bonanza, fails in the attempt, and dies broke.

Powell's political opposition ran the gamut of the Gilded Age—from provincial ignorance and local opportunism to greed and outright corruption. Hilary Herbert, a states rights senator from Alabama, proved a redoubtable opponent of all of Powell's surveys, fighting tenaciously for states rights and fiscal frugality. But the giant among such pygmies and the cause of Powell's eventual undoing was William "Big Bill" Stewart, burly senator from Nevada whom Stegner describes as "robust, aggressive, contentious, narrow, self-made, impatient . . . an indefatigable manipulator around the whiskey and cigars, a dragon whose cave was the smoke-filled room." It will be Stewart and his minions who kill Powell's dream of a scientifically and democratically managed West.

Stegner's account of Powell's hazardous expedition down the Colorado in 1869 opens the story of the major's career and is intended to mark the difficult beginnings of his passage from amateurism to professionalism. Like the naturalist John Muir and the botanist-sociologist Lester Ward whom he befriended, Powell was a son of the Middle Border, a self-educated provincial with wide-ranging curiosity but scant scientific training. A Civil War veteran who lost an arm at Shiloh, he was also a friend of General Grant's, and Grant supplied army rations for Powell's first Colorado River expedition. Slight of stature but wiry and toughened, a stern disciplinarian who drove himself harder than his men, Major Powell set off down the Green River in May 1869 with a "meager force" consisting of a handful of trappers in heavy, high-sided, unwieldy wooden boats difficult to line along the shore and nearly impossible to portage. For three months Powell and his men shot rapids, climbed canyon walls, lost precious baggage overboard, suffered desertions and went hungry before reaching their destination downriver. Despite Powell's quasi-military discipline and insatiable appetite for new facts, his expedition was less a scientific reconnaissance than a daily struggle for survival. Stegner's characterization is terse and to the point: "Nine men had plunged into the unknown from the last outpost of civilization in the Uinta Valley on the sixth of July, 1869. On August 30 six came out."

Stegner decided to re-create Powell's journey in detail in part because of the intrinsic drama of a harrowing adventure that made Powell famous but also in larger part in order to give readers an unforgettable impression of the terrain which he too knew well—claustrophobic canyons, the deafening roar of the rapids, towering unassailable cliffs on one of which the major nearly lost his life. Powell's vivid sense of scene and verbal shaping power produced depictions of landscape that were highly romantic yet compelling in their exact rendering of the forbidding country. A typical Powell description assembled from field notes for public consumption gives readers a panoramic view from on high of the juncture of the Colorado with the Green and Grand Rivers:

Below is the cañon, through which the Colorado runs. We can trace its course for miles, and at points catch glimpses of the river. From the northwest comes the Green, in a narrow, winding gorge. From the northeast comes the Grand, through a cañon that seems bottomless from where we stand. Away to the west are lines of cliff and ledges of rock—not such ledges as you may have seen where the quarryman splits his blocks, but ledges from which the gods might quarry mountains, that, rolled out on the plain below, would stand a lofty range, and not such cliffs as you may have seen where the swallow builds its nest, but cliffs where the soaring eagle is lost to view when he reaches the summit. Between us and the distant cliffs are strangely carved and pinnacled rocks of the *Toon-pin wu-near Tu-weap*. On the summit of the opposite wall of the cañon are rock forms we do not understand. Away to the east a group of eruptive mountains are seen—the Sierra La Sal. Their slopes are covered with pines, and deep gulches are flanked with great crags, and snow fields are seen near the summits. So the mountains are in uniform, green, gray, and silver. Wherever we look there is but a wilderness of rocks; deep gorges, where the rivers are lost below cliffs and towers and pinnacles; and ten thousand strangely carved forms in every direction; and beyond them mountains blending with the clouds.

Stegner frequently joins Powell and his fellow geologist Clarence Dutton on the terrain of the Plateau Province, describing in his own words vistas he clearly remembered and speculating on what wonders Powell might have seen.

He might have seen, with drifts of snow even yet unmelted on their cliffs, the southward thrusting edges of the Aquarius, Thousand Lake, perhaps even the distant rims of Fish Lake and the Wasatch Plateaus, basal-topped, flame-edged where they were eroded into cliffs. . . . He saw chocolate strata sculptured like organ pipes, a crumbling talus of blue-green shale, gray cliffs streaked with yellow, fierce outbreaks of red. In that maze cliffs swung and meandered and appeared far off hazed with distance across hollow valleys of unmitigated stone.

The interpretive center of Stegner's study of Powell consists of two chapters: "The Plateau Province," giving an account of Powell's scientific expeditions, and "Blueprint for a Dryland

Democracy," a summary of the major's famous *Report*. It is just here, Stegner explains, that "disinterested Science" intersects with "interested Politics." The Plateau Province, as Powell called it to distinguish it from the Arid Region's Park Province and the Great Basin Province, extends southwestward from the Uinta Mountains to the Colorado River and is mainly in Utah but spills over into Colorado on the east and Nevada on the west. Stegner, relying on Powell's investigations and his own firsthand impressions, pronounced it "scenically the most spectacular and humanly the least usable of all our regions." In the Arid Region and the Plateau Province in particular, Powell's uniformitarian conclusions and murky human history have "a poetic similarity." Here the earth rose and fell for millions of years beneath Carboniferous, Triassic, and Cretaceous oceans, then under the freshwater lakes of the Eocene age before being thrust up to be moulded by wind and water as river systems slice into it and constant winds sandblast it into fantastic shapes. "What had accumulated pebble by pebble and grain by grain, cemented with lime and silica, folding into itself the shells of sea life, scales of fishes, the compacted houses of corals, began to disintegrate again." Across millions of years geological forces have left only constant change. Knowledge of the human history of the Plateau Province, Stegner adds, is equally indistinct and offers only occasional glimpses of successive eras and epochs and their peoples—Anasazi in the dim recesses of time and more recently Shivwits, Kaibab, Navajo, Hopi, Paiute, whose languages Powell studied and whose ways he understood. Still, the human history of the Plateau Province remains as indistinct as its geological record. Sketchy accounts by early Spanish explorers and later fur traders and mountain men have yielded a mixture of folklore and fantasy concerning "an unknown and forbidding island" of rock.

Out of his two trips down the Colorado and the subsequent expeditions in the 1870s by his Geographical and Geological Survey of the Rocky Mountain Region came Powell's uniformitarian explanation of the Arid Region as the work of countless eons which slowly carved the present shape of the beautiful but forbidding canyon country. "We think of the mountains as forming clouds above their brows," Powell explained with a clarity and felicity which impressed his biographer, "but the clouds have formed the mountains. Great continental blocks are upheaved from beneath the sea by internal geologic forces. . . . Then the wandering clouds, the tempest-bearing clouds . . . with mighty power and wonderful skill carve out our valleys and canyons and fashion hills and cliffs and mountains."

Powell's Geographical and Geological Survey began as a ragtag operation funded by a meager $10,000 grant from Congress, and it competed with the more prestigious and well-heeled Fortieth Parallel Survey of Clarence King, Ferdinand Hayden's Survey of the Territories, and Army Captain George M. Wheeler's Survey West of the 100th Meridian. But from such unpromising beginnings would come Powell's classic *Report on the Lands of the Arid Region* in 1878. The report provided a needed corrective to the waste and corruption involved in the development and settlement of the arid West. American land policy in the Gilded Age was a travesty of intelligent and equitable planning. The Timber Culture Act (1873) and the subsequent Desert Land Act (1877), ostensibly drafted to assist individual small farmers and settlers, had exactly the reverse effect in benefiting speculators, big cattle outfits, mining syndicates, and timber companies. Powell's *Report* was designed to provide a scientific and democratic alternative for the Arid Region.

The key to Powell's plan for managing land that received less than 20 inches of rainfall annually—a region lying beyond the 100th meridian—was communal cooperation in settling seemingly unpromising lands. Inevitably the problem of living on such land reduced to understanding both the limits placed on it by nature and the needs, customs, practices, and values of the people who attempt to settle it. Regions, Powell and Stegner agreed, are marked not simply by nature but by an adaptive process called culture. And culture, both further understood, is itself an adaptive process that can be studied, planned, and implemented. From years spent researching Powell's ideas and career Stegner realized that both of them were primarily concerned with helping the small farmer and his family—just those people whose children and grandchildren the young Stegner had encountered in the Plateau Province. It occurred to the biographer as it had originally to his subject that in the management of scarce water throughout the Arid Region the Mormons had much to teach the rest of the world. And the lesson? Voluntary cooperation and communal management. Irrigable land constituted only 3.3 percent of the region, according to Powell's investigations. Powell realized that without water the standard homestead of 160 acres was virtually useless but that, once irrigated, it would be too much land for the single farmer to manage. Accordingly, he proposed an 80-acre homestead unit for irrigated farms but for adjoining pasturage farms 2,560 acres—four whole sections—needed to sustain grazing animals on native grasses. Big cattle outfits complained that even Powell's four sections would not be sufficient to feed a profitable herd of cattle, but Powell, like Stegner later, had most clearly in mind the needs of the small independent rancher-farmer, who in addition to an adequate amount of arable land would require a sufficient supply of water. Water was the key to the whole problem of settlement.

Solving the problem of an adequate supply of water required making two crucial changes: revising the system of riparian rights and installing programs for community management of irrigation projects in much the same fashion that Bernard DeVoto's grandfather, Samuel Dye, and his neighbors had cooperated in bringing water to the foothills of the Wasatch range. Traditional riparian rights to streams mandating the return of the water to the streambed by the owner made no sense in an arid country. Powell proposed—and Stegner appreciated the major's innovative genius—that each pasturage farm should have within its 2,560 acres some 20 acres of irrigable land complete with a water right which inhered in that land so farmers could raise their crops and the hay and alfalfa needed for winter stock. Arranging and dividing the land in the Arid Region in such fashion as to ensure scientific and democratic usage meant surveying and distributing it, not in standard rectangular parcels as was common east of the 100th meridian but according to the logic imposed by nature. This, in turn, meant redrawing sites for settlement and allowing farm plots to be as irregular as necessary in order to assure water frontage and thus irrigable soil. Powell's purpose, it was clear at the time and subsequently to Stegner, was to assure the West's little people, the independent farmers and their families, a decent living based on a sustainable way of life. To fail in this task would be to invite private water monopolies to take charge. Instead, Powell proposed and Stegner approved a plan to allow the settlers on the ground to decide how to divide their land into large pasturage farms and small irrigated plots.

Just here lay the revolutionary significance of Powell's proposals for Arid Region land management, which he insisted would be at once scientific and democratic. What Powell envisioned and what still held appeal for Stegner seventy-five years later was a managerial partnership with the federal government providing general oversight and local people collectively carrying out a policy of scientifically based land management. Powell wanted the general principles of land distribution established in Washington by the Coast and Geodetic Survey staffed by disinterested experts free from the influence of special interests and thus from political corruption. At the same time he sought to leave the actual implementation to the people on the ground who would apply the scientific principles intelligently and democratically. In short, Powell was proposing utopia. As Stegner commented after describing the intended workings of Powell's scheme, "It was so far beyond the social and economic thinking of the period that popularized the pork barrel as a national symbol and began the systematic gutting of the continent's resources and developed to its highest and most ruthless stage the competitive ruthlessness of American business, that it seems like the product of another land and another people." So it seemed to him in 1953, and so it still seems a half-century later. To an extent Powell's plan *was* the product of other societies and peoples, as Stegner knew full well. The idea of a community-managed common range—the *ejidos* Stegner had admired in *One Nation*—was the contribution of Spanish villagers in New Mexico. The other example of communal enterprise, less democratic but efficient nonetheless, was provided by the Mormons and their irrigation schemes, with which Samuel Dye and his neighbors had made the Wasatch desert bloom.

Powell's plan for the Arid Region, it was clear to Stegner, had encountered immediate opposition from the tribe of Gilpin with their inherited fantasies and phony individualism. More important, "It challenged too the men who were already beginning to ride like robber barons and kings over the public domain, and the corporations who were already, with Scottish and English and American capital, beginning to acquire those water-bearing half- and quarter-sections upon whose possession depended the control of range to support a cattle empire." In combination these vested interests defeated Major Powell.

Stegner gave over the rest of his study of Powell to a dramatic account of his battles with Congress, his eventual defeat and resignation. But he also closely examined Powell's philosophical writing, which he found abstruse, and his social ethics, with which he wholeheartedly agreed. Labor, whether of the mind or body, Powell told the Anthropological Society of Washington, had become so interconnected in an age of consolidation that inevitably every man works for some other man. "He struggles directly to benefit others, that he may indirectly but ultimately benefit himself." He cited his own career as an example: his scientific work undertaken together with the investigative community he had founded made him "master of the world" but at the same time "every man's servant." "So are we all—servants to many masters and master of many servants." Stegner, convinced that his own moderate liberalism depended on just such a widely shared social ethic, considered it Powell's chief legacy to the twentieth century.

In his concluding chapter, "The Inheritance," Stegner surveyed subsequent environmental planning developments and imagined that Powell returned to the American scene in the mid-twentieth century to pronounce his verdict. Powell would discover ground gained and ground lost and realize that however much had changed in the fifty years since his death, the battle between the forces of unchecked development and scientific management had not waned.

The forces he fought all during his public life are, as of 1953, not only still there but active and aggressive. The agencies that he helped consolidate still persist in division and antagonism. The private interests that he feared might monopolize land and water in the West are still there, still trying to do just that. And the scientific solutions to western problems are still fouled up by the Gilpins, by the doubletalk of Western members of Congress, by political pressures from oil or stock or land or water companies, by the obfuscations of press agents and the urgings of lobbyists. In 1953 a public land policy that a few years before [during the New Deal] had looked reasonably consistent and settled was in danger of complete overturn.

In assessing Powell's contributions to contemporary conservation and land management Stegner emphasized the weaknesses and failures of the various federal agencies that Powell had either helped found or approved: the infighting between the Reclamation Bureau and the Army Corps of Engineers; the cross-purposes of the Departments of Interior and Agriculture; the squabbling between the Park Service and the Forest Service, both of them bent on building an empire. All of which was to admit that administrative government from Washington had proved to be no panacea. Then there was Congress itself, mouthpiece for selfish local interests both big and small, which were determined to take huge bites out of the national forests and public lands all the while railing against "absentee landlordism" in Washington. Nevada's Senator McCarran, "Big Bill" Stewart "come again," with his grip on the congressional pocketbook, was perhaps the nation's most formidable foe of land planning and conservation. Finally, Stegner pointed out, Powell would be forced to rethink the whole question of hydroelectric power, massive dam-building programs, and the engineers' dreams of redesigning the entire West in their own interests.

In view of these checkered developments, what might Major Powell be expected to do should he be revived in the year 1953? In answering the question Stegner spoke his own concerns and announced his own intentions. "He might join the Sierra Club and other conservation groups in deploring some proposed and 'feasible' dams such as that in Echo Park below the mouth of the Yampa." Powell would have come to understand that wildlife preservation, wilderness protection, managed and monitored recreation sites—issues just beginning to surface in his own day—frequently outweigh the values of irrigation and power. With his penchant for investigating thoroughly the Major would realize that dams, for example, are not an unmitigated blessing, that they silt up and make ugly landscapes behind them. And he would have concluded with his biographer that "men had better look a long way ahead when they begin tampering with natural forces."

Finally, what Powell recognized in his time and what his populist disciples Bernard DeVoto and Wallace Stegner were learning in theirs was the principle of a national commons and the absolute necessity of preserving it for all Americans. All three men knew from bitter experience that private interests, whether in timber, minerals, or cattle, as Stegner put it bluntly, "could not be trusted or expected to take care of the land or conserve its resources for the use of future generations." It came down, then, to a matter of values and the urgent need in a postwar age of environmental heedlessness to educate, organize, and activate national public opinion. This task, Stegner agreed with DeVoto, now fell to a new agent, the enlightened and energized public intellectual: novelist, short story writer, biographer but also environmental spokesman. In 1953, the year *Beyond the Hundredth*

Meridian appeared, Stegner published an article in the *Reporter*, "One-Fourth of the Nation: Public Land and Itching Fingers," and a year later a short piece for the *New Republic*, "Battle for the Wilderness." With the long-simmering controversy over plans for a dam inside Dinosaur National Monument now reaching a political boil, the issue between developers and conservationists had finally been joined. His old friend in Cambridge was right: they must go to work in earnest.

Land

Overleaf: The Inner Gorge. (From *The Exploration of the Colorado River and Its Canyons*, J. W. Powell, 1895.)

I 〜

Bernard DeVoto and Wallace Stegner joined the environmental crusade following World War II as loyal and knowledgeable conservationists. The original conservation movement, as the historian Samuel P. Hays has explained, differed from the new environmentalism in impulse and intention, purpose and process. Conservation, which dated from the turn of the century, was essentially a top-down movement, a producerist program designed to improve efficiency and eliminate waste in the use of the nation's natural resources. The conservation agenda was the handiwork of a rising generation of experts and trained professionals in government and big business alike who preached and practiced scientific management and what they called "wise use." Conservationists relied on expertise and training, surveys, pilot projects, and fact-finding. They championed administrative government and staffed independent commissions freed from legislative control. Lacking a genuine ideology, they examined nature with a purely practical eye and invoked the need to save at least part of it for future generations. Versed in the techniques of Theodore Roosevelt's Progressivism, many of conservation's practitioners later joined his cousin Franklin's New Deal. Stegner and DeVoto numbered themselves among the supporters of the New Deal's several conservation programs. Both men agreed on the primacy of fact-finding, admired the seemingly disinterested scientists who practiced it, and agreed on the uses of federal power to protect the

American land. Their postwar recruitment to environmentalism stemmed from these shared values.

As a son of the West and supporter of the New Deal's land programs DeVoto was securely attached to its producerist assumptions. The New Deal initially appeared to him as the logical culmination of the doctrine of efficiency, and he generally approved its accomplishments. It had substituted sustainable yields for the unthinking liquidation of American resources. It had checked soil erosion, helped restore rundown rural areas of the country, launched reclamation projects, and furthered economic recovery all across the nation. In the Arid Region, New Deal measures had also built the base for Western industrial development which World War II completed. If there was a law of progress at work in American history, then the New Deal seemingly provided the needed proof.

Yet history, as DeVoto studied and wrote it, offered no such assurances. In fact, from the perspective of an avowed conservationist, American history frequently appeared cyclical with the same contending forces across generations lined up against each other under the opposing banners of conservation and liquidation. As he prepared to confront the latest liquidators of his West DeVoto sought to put them in historical perspective. The West, he had argued for some time, had always been the exploited colony of Eastern business and finance, the victim of a one-way developmental process siphoning off Western wealth to fill Eastern coffers. This history of regional exploitation, first compiled by Walter Prescott Webb, was DeVoto's and Stegner's as well. For DeVoto the story began with his fabled Mountain Men bought and bilked by Eastern entrepreneurs. In the decades following the Civil War the liquidation of Western resources accelerated with the arrival of mining syndicates, lumber combines, and cattle empires, all financed with Eastern money and encouraged by a servile government at both the state and national levels. Thus the present postwar attempt of the grazing interests in the West to take back what they persisted in calling "their land" bore all the marks of a repeat performance.

The grazing industry in the West had never been happy with even the minimal regulations provided by the Taylor Act during the early years of the New Deal. Now flush with wartime profits, cattlemen—large outfits and small independents—banded together with sheep ranchers in an attempt to remove all grazing lands from the Bureau of Land Management and redistribute them to the states and ultimately to private owners at nominal cost. They also sought to have all Forest Service holdings reclassified so that grazing lands inside the national forests would also be returned to the states. "In other words," Wallace Stegner explained in recounting his friend's bold opposition to the cattlemen's proposed landgrab, "they wanted to liquidate the Bureau of Land Management and emasculate the Forest Service and gain ownership of a princely but fragile domain that belonged to all Americans." In his lead attack on the cattle industry DeVoto put the point more succinctly. "This is your land we are talking about." Already by 1947 the grazing interests, with Nevada's Senator Pat McCarran as their point man, had eliminated the docile Grazing Service by merging it with the remnants of the old General Land Office as part of an enfeebled Bureau of Land Management whose budget and staff McCarran proceeded to cut drastically. This was the attack on the public realm which DeVoto determined to block on his return from his tour of the West.

The grazing industry's attempted landgrab, as DeVoto called it, was part of a larger crisis of federalism in the decade following the end of the war. In what appeared to be a counterrevolutionary reaction against federal power which had expanded greatly during the New Deal and war years, local and regional business interests, aided and abetted by a resurgent Republican Party, now sought to dismantle the regulatory apparatus of the national economy. By 1947 it appeared to apprehensive observers like DeVoto that the traditional conservation movement was in danger of being overrun by hostile special interests in mining, grazing, and lumbering. Cattlemen had already appropriated for themselves the phrase "wise use," once the motto of Gifford Pinchot's conservation movement, and were now employing it as a cover for unchecked private development. Now after the war it seemed that conservationists, stripped of their original rationale, lacked the strength and the will to face down their enemies hellbent, as DeVoto suspected, on the liquidation of the entire West. Conservation, it was clear to him, was in dire need of a new ideology of national authority directly responsive to the popular will. This doctrine of a national commons shared by all Americans was precisely what he now decided to give it.

In urging his readers to follow his example by walking the bounds of their joint property DeVoto was inviting them to see for themselves the extent of the national domain and to enjoy it as their land. "Land belonging to all the people," was the key concept connecting an updated populism with a postwar consumerism and tourism. DeVoto admitted to no mystical appreciation of wildness. As a native Westerner who had grown up in the foothills of the Wasatch Range, he enjoyed but did not worship what he continued to call "scenery." He viewed nature with the same unsentimental eye he used to examine the rest of American life. For him it came down finally to a question of ethics—a preservationist creed similar to Aldo Leopold's land ethic but connected to a democratic populist belief in the importance of open access to public land vouchsafed to all Americans. The history of the

Western land held a more mundane appeal for him than it did for Wallace Stegner. He made his successive trips through the West retracing the route of Lewis and Clark and following the trails taken by immigrants to Oregon as an unapologetic tourist who reported to "Easy Chair" readers on the quality of roadside diners, motels, road conditions, and local hospitality. Landscape *spoke* to him but from an emotional distance with little of the aesthetic immediacy that Stegner experienced and expressed so directly.

Connected to this public inheritance were not only rights of access and enjoyment but also responsibilities including a vigorous defense of their land against private encroachment. DeVoto's tour of the West had also opened his eyes to a whole network of national parks and forests, all staffed and managed by dedicated professionals, frequently against the open opposition of local interests. This corps of loyal public servants needed all the support it could get in checking developmental invaders. Interest-group government had bred a giant contingent of corporate lobbyists hired by special interests like the cattlemen to invade Washington and badger Congress for special dispensation. And Congress, which DeVoto had recently touted as a countervailing force to a powerful executive, now appeared the captive of those special interests who were dispatching their agents to Capitol Hill, publishing heavily biased trade journals, and manipulating local opinion back home. DeVoto decided to join the fray as an unpaid lobbyist for the Forest and Park Services. Here was an expanded role for the postwar public intellectual with a yen for investigative journalism. From friends in the Forest Service and Western conservation groups he had learned of the intention of the grazing interests to dismantle the agency. Primed with a whole new batch of facts, he fired off what was to be the most famous of his *Harper's* articles, "The West

Against Itself," the first of some forty pieces he would write on environmental issues in the next nine years.

"The West Against Itself" marked a broadening of DeVoto's outlook on the environment. Early parts of the essay rehearsed—but with a difference—his by-now-familiar complaints against Eastern exploitation of Western resources. A new combination of Eastern money and Western greed now confronted the Forest Service with regional demands for the return of what ranchers deceptively called "their land." A central section of DeVoto's analysis dealt with these miscreants and their intentional misreading of the law and American history. But at this point he turned to consider the ecological consequences of overgrazing and the rapid ruination of the public domain. He readily admitted that the stockmen were by no means the only or even the most destructive liquidators of Western resources. That dubious honor probably belonged to the mining industry with the lumber companies a close second. Both of them followed the cardinal rule of spoilers everywhere: "You clean up and get out—and you don't give a damn." Still, it was the grazing interests—the cattle and sheep outfits, big and little—who formed the vanguard of the attack on the public domain, and DeVoto accordingly concentrated his fire on them. Anyone with the slightest acquaintance with American history, he announced, would realize that "the cattlemen never owned more than a mere one per cent of the range they grazed, and they don't own it now: it belongs to you and me."

The most urgent problem needing fixing was overgrazing on the public lands and its effect on watersheds. Most of the major watersheds of the West lay inside the boundaries of the Taylor Act lands, the national forests, or the national parks. Overgrazing destroyed these lands, sometimes gradually, more often quickly, and this was what the Forest Service was trying to prevent by limiting the size of the herds. For their part, the cattlemen and sheep grazers wanted to shovel the West into its rivers.

> Stream beds choke with silt and floods spread over the rich fields on the slopes and in the bottoms, always impairing and sometimes destroying them. Dams and canals and reservoirs silt up, decline in efficiency, have to be repaired at great expense, cannot be fully restored. Fields gully, soils blow away. Flash floods kill productive land, kill livestock, kill human beings, sometimes kill communities.

Did his readers require proof? Then consider the recent summer storm that descended on the tiny Mormon town of Mount Pleasant, Utah, and sent a river of mud thick as cement pouring down the hills along gulches and straight through the main street carrying rocks and boulders with it. "The range above town had been overgrazed and the storm waters which would have been retained by healthy land could not be retained by the sick, exhausted land."

Pressure from the grazing interests prevailed upon the House Committee on Public Lands to authorize a subcommittee chaired by Wyoming Congressman Frank A. Barrett to hold hearings throughout the intermountain west on the restrictive grazing policies of the Forest Service. DeVoto recognized a put-up job when he saw it and reacted accordingly. Using the multivolume report of the subcommittee, he reconstructed the sequence of hearings held in Billings, Montana; Rawlins, Wyoming; Salt Lake City; Ely, Nevada; and elsewhere. With the overbearing Barrett firmly ensconced in the chair, the hearings had been a farce from the outset, rigged in favor of the enemies of the Forest Service. Barrett barred or shut off testimony from the Forest Service's supporters and closed the record to their protestations. Wherever possible he had stacked the hearings with raucous cattlemen and allowed them to shout down their opponents. The subcommittee also lined up ringers and public relations representatives. It spent only a part of a single day actually visiting the national forests. It refused to consult reports of the Forest Service, and rushed into print with its own report, which predictably recommended dissolution of the agency. But in the chaotic sessions in Ely, Nevada, Barrett and his minions overplayed their hand. One of the members of the subcommittee, having argued belligerently for the transfer of land from the Forest Service, made a preposterous claim which was becoming common in the opening days of the Cold War. He likened the activities of the Forest Service to Soviet Russia. While loyal Americans were gearing up to fight Soviet communism abroad, the congressman warned, others were busy building "that very same system" in the West. To protect the ranges, it seemed, amounted to sedition.

Such idiocy simply furnished meat for DeVoto's healthy appetite for controversy, and he was quick to pounce on the subcommittee's report. Dismissing such comments as "nonsense" and condemning the mind behind them as "grotesque," he turned from such "curiosa" to what he saw as the "really dangerous irresponsibility" of the stockgrowers' refusal to admit that overgrazing damages the forage, the land, and the watersheds. The only corrective to this perverse denial of scientific evidence was "the force of the ballot" since no amount of proof or appeals to long-term values would convince the stockmen. If Westerners could not control an ignorant minority, then the rest of the country would have to do the job. Although Truman's secretary of agriculture rejected recommendations for a moratorium on cuts in grazing permits, DeVoto knew the stockmen would be back. Already in 1948 there were signs of renewed activity, and they would bear constant watching. By themselves, he admitted, the grazing interests could not carry the day against a determined Truman administration, but that was not the point. The real danger lay elsewhere and was twofold. "The attack on the Forest Service is only one part of an unceasing, many-sided effort to discredit all conservation bureaus of government, to discredit conservation itself." Antienvironmentalists, moreover, were well heeled and eager to join forces: money and the means of influence were already in place. Meanwhile the consumption of natural resources inside as well as outside the public domain had increased astronomically. "If the interests that lust to get at them should form an effective combination they could bring the United States to the verge of catastrophe in a single generation." The threat, as he repeated regularly now, was not Western but national. Public pressure on the politicians offered the only hope of preventing further raids on the people's lands, and to them he presently directed his own attention.

In brushing aside DeVoto as an Eastern busybody and ignorant meddler in Western affairs his enemies seriously underestimated their man—at least in the beginning. DeVoto had reveled in controversy all his life, relishing nothing so much as a good verbal brawl and delighting in pummeling his opponents into submission. He was fully prepared, therefore, when complaints, threats, and insults came pouring into *Harper's* editorial offices. When the editor of the Denver *Post*, himself a transplanted Easterner, misrepresented DeVoto's views in opposing the Echo Dam project, he received an immediate demand for a correction accompanied by a question addressed to the "native Westerner from Roseville, Illinois." "Do you read the texts you quote, misunderstand them, or merely misrepresent them?" Then, after restating his position on the need for the West to conserve water, he closed with the reminder that "repulsive emigré that I am, I understand that necessity better than, apparently, the *Post* does." Again, replying to a complaint from an aggrieved stockman, he accused the grazing industry of refusing to conduct its business "on any level above imbecility" and topped his indictment with the suggestion that rather than eliminating the buffalo, "it would be simpler, less expensive, and more hopeful to shoot cattlemen." He demanded a retraction from a spokesman for the Wyoming Stock-Growers Association whose remarks he considered "false, defamatory, and libelous" and issued a warning: "If you do not care to retract them, do you choose to stand on them and have them tested legally?" And not long before he died in 1955 he received an "infuriated and sophomoric letter" from a public relations man for the lumber industry who threatened to come to Boston and punch him in the nose. DeVoto reminded his correspondent that "we have sophomores here too, and if you insist on behaving like one, you will end in jail."

These regular forays into investigative journalism now began to point the finger at politicians like the Republican aspirant for the presidency in 1948, Minnesota's Harold Stassen, who had sought Western political support by calling for a "major revision of public lands policy" and insisting that "there is too much public land now." Stung by DeVoto's comment in a review of Gifford Pinchot's *Breaking New Ground* that Stassen was one of the new breed of Republicans kowtowing to the grazing interests, Stassen protested and received in return a six-page, densely packed justification of DeVoto's criticism. DeVoto punctuated his letter with frequent "you must knows" indicating a string of attacks on the public lands. "Either you know these things," DeVoto concluded his lecture, "as nearly everyone does, and have given them the support of a man who intends to be President of the United States if he can make the grade, or you don't know them and are running for Presidential nomination and committing yourself in ignorance of them. In either case conservationists must speak out."

Montana's Democratic Senator Mike Mansfield fared scarcely better. Mansfield was an enthusiastic supporter of a bill to authorize the construction of Glacier View Dam inside Glacier National Park. In an article in the July 24, 1950, issue of the *Saturday Evening Post* DeVoto had argued strenuously against the project, which Mansfield was attempting to promote. Mansfield complained to *Post* editor Ben Hibbs, who passed the letter on to DeVoto, who sent a bristling retort back to the senator. Mansfield's statements supporting construction, DeVoto reminded him, were at variance with all of the facts compiled by the Department of Interior, the National Park Service, and various conservation groups. "What you say is not only contrary to the facts but exceedingly disingenuous." As for Mansfield's statement that man, animals, natural curiosities, and the timber industry would all benefit from Glacier View Dam, DeVoto dismissed the assertion as "simple nonsense unworthy of you."

The presidential election of 1952, which ushered in Eisenhower Republicanism, turned DeVoto into an intensely active Democrat. A former Northwestern student of his, George Ball, introduced him to Adlai Stevenson, the party's standard-bearer in the '52 election. Stevenson was a lukewarm conservationist at best, but he was nevertheless responsive to DeVoto's lectures, and for his part DeVoto was convinced that the Illinois governor was the answer to a conservationist's prayer. Never one one to do things by halves, he quickly jumped on the Stevenson bandwagon. "*Use* me!" he insisted to the campaign staff and offered to write the planks on public land policy for the party together with a conservation brief and speeches for its candidate. Stevenson later told Wallace Stegner that DeVoto was too good a writer and too set in his views to sound like anyone else, and that he had used the proffered material sparingly. As the campaign progressed

DeVoto's initial optimism faded even as he continued to bombard his candidate with free advice. He told his friend Garrett Mattingly that he had urged Stevenson to challenge Eisenhower's competence "on the ground that he is ignorant of the structure, functions, and mechanisms of the federal government." Stevenson chose to ignore this advice.

The DeVoto-Stevenson friendship survived the Democratic defeat: both the candidate and his loyal followers knew that he would in all probability try again in 1956. Thus assured, DeVoto continued to instruct his man on the crucial importance of the national forests as the very foundation on which Western growth and prosperity depended. "I know that everybody on God's earth is pressing advice on you and making demands on your time. But there is no bigger domestic problem than this one and no brighter opportunity for the Democrats." To drive home his point he invited Stevenson to visit a national forest in Montana with him, courtesy of the Region One office of the Forest Service. Stevenson accepted, and the two men, accompanied by DeVoto's young doctor friend, spent two days in the mountains where Stevenson received a hands-on lesson in conservation. Subsequently DeVoto urged on his new friend a comprehensive program for the West. "Conservation thinking suffers from repetitiousness, hidebound tradition, and an inability to realize that the world of 1950 frequently requires different answers from those that were satisfactory in 1900." He would not live to see the change.

There were two powerful constraints on environmental thinking in the early fifties: McCarthyism and Republican developmentalism. McCarthyism spread fear and hatred across the country, poisoning the atmosphere needed to discuss resource policy. And Eisenhower appointees sought to curb or remove federal regulation of land and resource use. DeVoto's war against censorship and repression was a long-standing one. It had begun with his dislike of the Mormon practice of shutting down on opinions deemed contrary to the Church's received wisdom. It flared during the Scopes trial and again in the Sacco-Vanzetti tragedy. Now after the Second World War as censors shifted their attention from wartime security to literature they considered pornographic or otherwise offensive, DeVoto issued yet another call to arms. The pseudo-historical novel *Forever Amber* was tasteless, he agreed, but harmless, as was the clinical sex in Edmund Wilson's *Memoirs of Hecate County*. Lillian Smith's *Strange Fruit*, however, a hard-hitting critique of American racism, offended only bigots. But all three books together with others pouring out of the commercial press needed defending against would-be censors. "The place to fight censorship," DeVoto announced, "is whatever place it appears in, for anyone who denies us access to error by that act denies us access to truth as well." When a congressional select committee issued a report recommending censoring paperbacks and comic books, DeVoto attacked its reasoning as "mendacious, ignorant, preposterous." "It may be news to you that the blonde in her underwear who adorns the cover of *Silas Marner* at the newsstand has undermined American society, but you have worse to learn." Worse was the opinion of the select committee that the Founding Fathers' protection of liberty was now in danger of "being transmuted by unscrupulous persons into license."

But a political urge to conformity in the early years of the Cold War ran deeper than an occasional assault on literature, art, and film, as the House Un-American Activities Committee (HUAC) presently made clear. During Commencement Week, 1949, HUAC asked some seventy colleges and universities across the country to submit course readings in all social science and literature courses. DeVoto rushed to the defense of intellectual freedom and denounced those institutions that had complied. The next step, he warned quite correctly, was to rid college faculties of known communists and to aid the FBI in ferreting them out. He had announced to the FBI that he would stop providing information on his acquaintances, a practice which was turning Americans into a nation of informers. It had already gone too far, and the country was now divided into the hunters and the hunted. The spirit of the Salem Witch Trials was drifting across the land. There would be no more cooperation from him with snoopers from the FBI or anywhere else. "I like a country where it's nobody's damned business what magazines anyone reads, what he thinks, whom he has cocktails with. . . . We had that kind of country only a little while ago and I'm for getting it back."

DeVoto had not changed his mind about communism, and he had little patience with the former party member who confessed his sin and told all. "Understand, I am right now *because* I was wrong then," the ex-communist appeared to argue. "Where, for God's sake," DeVoto demanded, "was he when they were distributing minds?" Luckily the number of intellectuals who became communists in the thirties had been small even though "high-church Republican politics finds a useful technique in representing it to have been enormous."

More ominous to DeVoto than communism in its decrepit state was the sudden appearance of Joe McCarthy, an "unspeakable" paranoid and his "licensor," Robert Taft, who was in need of an intelligence test. The problem wasn't subversion, as conservative critics charged, but lay in another direction—in the reactionary views of two-thirds of the bankers of the country, three-quarters of its newspaper owners, 85 percent of the heads of big businesses, and a full 90 percent of the nation's university trustees. After tabulating the statistics that defined his own politics, he announced himself half a Mugwump, 60 percent a New Dealer, 90 percent Populist, and a dirt road historian to boot. He denounced McCarthy as a Typhoid Mary, "the carrier of an infection far more dangerous to our political institutions than any other decay now apparent in them."

DeVoto also kept his eye on congressional investigative committees and their several reports, in part because of the threats some of them posed to civil liberties, in larger part because here was where the attacks on the Forest Service and the Park Service were originating under Eisenhower Republicanism. He kept unearthing strange items like the 432-page Reece Committee Report, which purported to find the Carnegie, Rockefeller, and Ford Foundations riddled with communists and fellow travelers. "Crack-brained" and "dishonest" was DeVoto's verdict on the committee's findings, but also dangerous and genuinely subversive of American liberties. Not merely congressional right-wingers but the activities of superpatriots everywhere received the patented DeVoto response. In Connecticut the Veterans of Foreign Wars was calling for a national witch hunt; in Massachusetts, the American Legion was raising the same false alarm. In his warning he quoted President Eisenhower as saying he doubted whether much could be done to prevent people from compiling and using such lists of supposed subversives. Didn't the president understand, DeVoto scoffed, that in all these cases there was no identifiable accuser, no specific individual or group to confront? Accusers were faceless "half-wits" who passed their suspicions on to congressional "rumpots" who in turn put them into some congressional file.

When his victims attempted to fire back, DeVoto simply dipped deeper into his reserve of ammunition. When, for example, he pointed to the foolishness of the Gathings Committee, which had estimated the number of known communists and leftists in northwestern Pennsylvania at 67,900, one of its members indulged in a bit of guilt-by-association maneuvering by noting that DeVoto's defense of civil liberties had been applauded by the *Daily Worker*. DeVoto dismissed the congressman as a "hit-and-run defamer" and his insinuations as "deliberate and dishonest."

As early as 1948 it had become clear that the land-grabbers in the West had the blessing and the backing of the Republican Party. Harold Stassen and Thomas R. Dewey, party hopefuls both, declared in favor of scaling back federal interference with the rights of the states and reviewing federal land policies. All of the attempts to reduce the scale of Forest Services activities enjoyed the support of Republicans. As early as 1940 DeVoto had pointed out that traditionally it had been the Democratic Party—Jefferson's in 1800, Jackson's in 1828, Cleveland's, Wilson's, and FDR's in that order—which had restored Pareto's equilibrium to a political and financial system thrown out of balance by "primarily those associated with concentrations of economic or financial power." This appeared to be the present postwar situation as Republicans declared their intention to roll back federal regulations, and Democrats struggled to preserve the gains of the New Deal with Truman's Fair Deal. By 1952 DeVoto's partisanship was open and declared. The Republican platform that year contained a plank drafted by General Pat Hurley at the behest of the grazing interests urging a return to the party's "traditional public land policy." Hurley's draft went on to call for "opportunity for ownership by citizens to promote the highest land use and the elimination of bureaucratic favoritism."

Just *which* "Republican tradition" did current party leaders favor,

DeVoto demanded to know. The tradition of Theodore Roosevelt, Gifford Pinchot, WJ McGee and the pioneer conservationists, all of them Republican? Or the tradition of venality and degradation inherited by Republicans Richard Ballinger and Albert Fall from an earlier generation of spoilsmen? To answer his own question he offered a substitute to the Hurley plank:

> We pledge the Republican Party to strip the Forest Service of its power to regulate and administer its grazing ranges, and to transfer that power to the present holders of grazing permits. We favor legislation which will put grazing, a subsidiary use of national forests and in dollars the least important one, in a position superior and adverse to other uses such as lumbering, mining, irrigation, municipal and industrial water supply, watershed protection, hunting, fishing, camping and the public interest in general. We demand that there be no protection of ranges or watersheds by reducing the number of stock now permitted to graze on them or by any change we do not like in the terms on which grazing permits are held. We also demand an Act of Congress that will give the present holders of grazing permits a legally vested hold on the national forests, will enable them to keep other stockmen out of the forests, will authorize them to set grazing fees as they see fit, and will empower them to formulate and enforce their own regulations without regard to the public interest.

Eisenhower set the tone and the direction of the incoming administration in calling for a new "partnership" between government and developmental forces as a replacement for intrusive federal management. Under the Democrats, the president declared, federal agencies had been so deeply involved in water management that they had done everything "but come in and wash the dishes for the housewife." Beware of "super-government," Ike warned, interfering with local interests and mandating development from Washington. Let's strike a deal, he urged, "bringing in the federal government, not as a boss, not as your dictator, but as a friendly partner ready to help and get its long nose out of your business." In other words, snorted DeVoto, "get out and send more money."

Conservationists, still relatively dispersed and disunited in 1953, viewed the Republican ascendance with an odd mixture of apprehension and apathy. Conservation organizations and their developmental opponents alike awaited intently the appointment of a new secretary of the interior. Eisenhower himself had warned about "creeping socialism" within the department, and his appointment of former businessman and governor of Oregon Douglas McKay brought into office a business-minded administrator with a strong distaste for government spending and budget deficits and a permissive tolerance of lumber, oil, and mining interests. Trees, he assured lumbermen in the Northwest, were simply a crop to be grown and harvested. "I have no sympathy for those mistaken souls who preach our forests should be socialized and turned over . . . for . . . stewardship," he announced in explaining his preference for "constructive" private ownership. Oregon's Democratic Senator Wayne Morse warned the conservation community that McKay was really "a well-recognized stooge of the tidelands thieves, the private utility gang, and other selfish interests which place material values above human values." McKay soon proved Morse's judgment correct as DeVoto was quick to realize.

McKay retained Park Service Commissioner Conrad Wirth but forced the resignation of the Bureau of Reclamation's feisty Michael Straus, who had appeared willing to dam every river in the country. On leaving, Straus reminded McKay that Reclamation had flourished under the Square Deal, the New Deal, and the Fair Deal, but he wondered how it would now fare under the Big Deal with corporate ownership. Conservationists, for their part, followed developments within the bureau warily, for it was well known by this time that its engineers were ready at a moment's notice to build a dam inside Dinosaur National Monument at Echo Park as a key component of the Upper Colorado Storage Project, an ill-conceived scheme for constructing a string of dams up and down the Colorado River.

The controversy over Echo Park Dam touched off by the Upper Colorado Storage Project had been simmering for several years by the time of Eisenhower's election. The project was the creation of a variety of regional interests, both Republican and Democratic, calling for water and power development as crucial to Western economic growth. The Bureau of Reclamation had geared up in earnest on the Storage Project in 1946, hoping to cash in on the New Deal's initial investment in dam building and resource planning. Throughout the Depression and war years both DeVoto and Stegner had been strong supporters of the bureau's work. As late as 1946, following a tour of his home country, Stegner could write of the wonders of Hoover (then Boulder) Dam, that "sweeping cliff of concrete, those impetuous elevators, the labyrinth of tunnels, the huge power stations," celebrating it as a monument "peculiarly American." But in a later article in the same series he expressed concern over the bureau's apparently irrepressible urge to develop the region by building dams down the entire length of the Colorado River. And by 1950 his travels through the Plateau Province and a growing appreciation of the Park Service forced him to reconsider and question the advantages of indiscriminate dam building. The rocks and canyons, he noted, might be safe from "people with paint cans" and an urge to deface natural beauty but not necessarily from the engineers with a yen to improve it. At just this time DeVoto was also executing a 180-degree turn on the issue of dams along the Colorado. His appointment to the advisory board of the Park Service had opened new channels of information on the ambitious plans of the Bureau of Reclamation and the Army Corps of Engineers. When he learned of the bureau's development scheme for constructing a main stem dam at Echo Park inside Dinosaur National Monument, he turned fiercely against it.

The key to the bureau's development scheme was Echo Park Dam and another at Split Mountain, both sites square in the middle of Dinosaur National Monument, whose pristine wilderness conservationists were determined to preserve. The chief problem for the opponents of the dams was that back in 1941 the then director of the Park Service, Nelson Drury, had signed a memorandum with the Bureau of Reclamation seemingly agreeing to construction. Although by 1948, when DeVoto entered the debate, the Park Service seemed reconciled, however reluctantly, to the construction of the two dams, private conservation groups were not similarly inclined. The National Parks Association, the Wilderness Society, and the Izaak Walton League among others condemned the project outright. Local promoters of the dams, fuming at growing public opposition in the East to their project, took their cue from the Vernal, Utah, *Express,* whose editor lashed out at city "nature lovers" and warned them that if they wanted a good fight, "there is no group in the world that likes one better than the Westerner." Fair enough, DeVoto replied, choose your weapon!

DeVoto's vigorous championing of the Park and Forest Services had earned him in 1948 an appointment to the National Park Advisory Board, an assignment he welcomed because it kept him abreast of Washington politics and in touch with his widening network of friends in the various regional offices. Now fully committed to park and forest preservation, he began to seek a wider readership than the pages of *Harper's* afforded. He sounded out editors of such popular magazines as *Holiday*, the *American*, *Colliers*, and the *Saturday Evening Post*, all of whom remained chary of the partisanship and polemic for which he was famous. Only *Woman's Day*, under the able direction of Mabel Souvine, continued to accept most of what he offered it. More typical was a returned manuscript on the High Country from *Holiday* accompanied by four pages of suggested improvements. "No doubt there are writers who would be willing to attempt the piece you outline," he replied to the editor, "but I am not one of them." To his agent he fired off a volley of complaints concerning the proposed improvements:

> Go easy about sleeping on the ground—Jesus Christ! Don't mention the fact that the slopes are steep if you're writing about mountain climbing; don't mention the fact that you sometimes sweat if you're writing about playing tennis. "Alluring vacation resort"—God damn! I'm telling them what this country is like. . . . Why doesn't the crazy bastard get some copywriter from his advertising department to write what he wants.

Wherever he sent a piece on preservation of the environment, it seemed, it came back with a rejection slip. Environmental issues were not yet very high on the American reading public's agenda at midcentury, and it would take the combined efforts of DeVoto and his friend Wallace Stegner to help raise the ranking.

By the time President Eisenhower publicly endorsed the Reclamation Bureau's Upper Colorado River Storage Project,

DeVoto had been on record as opposed to it for some time. He was also opposed to building Glacier View Dam inside Glacier National Park, and he argued strenuously against the Pick-Sloan project on the upper Missouri River despite a hugely enjoyable two-week excursion from the river's headwaters to its mouth as the guest of the chief of the Army Corps of Engineers, General S.G. Sturgis. He was convinced that in the fifties the greatest threat to the national parks and forests came from the Army Corps of Engineers and the Bureau of Reclamation. In a friendly letter to General Sturgis thanking him for his hospitality he proceeded to restate his objections to putting short-term sectional interests ahead of the national interest which, he admitted, was not sufficiently represented against clamorous local and regional voices that drowned it out. In this sense the New Deal's task in pulling together a dispersed and diffused American society remained uncompleted. There were frequent congressional committee meetings at the grass roots, he admitted, but those pitted fully informed and well-prepared local interests against "only the weak and usually belated opposition of a few conservation organizations, whose membership is small, whose voice is feeble, and whose treasure is almost nonexistent." Outside the West in the early fifties most Americans knew virtually nothing about the massive projects planned by the Bureau of Reclamation and the Army Corps of Engineers who competed vigorously against each other for lucrative contracts. DeVoto was forced to admit that Congress, which he had once valued so highly, was filled with logrollers and back-scratchers, and could offer no resistance to such boondoggles as ill-advised dam projects. "There is simply no way of making this criticism effective. If the public interest is endangered, there is simply no way of taking action to prevent the danger." What was needed, he told the general, was an independent investigatory commission empowered to evaluate costs and benefits. But until that distant time came it fell to conservationists to bestir themselves, organize, and publish.

The most vulnerable part of the national domain in 1950 was Dinosaur National Monument in northeast Utah straddling the state line with Colorado. Here at the juncture of the Green and Yampa Rivers the Bureau of Reclamation, backed by clamorous local support, planned to build two dams: one at Split Mountain and a second at Echo Park's spectacular Steamboat Rock. Echo Park had been described by one of the Park Service's consulting landscape architects as "geologically and scenically . . . probably the most extraordinary feature in the entire monument," the juncture of the two rivers exceeding "in sheer loveliness" anything in the area. With his recently acquired insider's information on Park Service plans and problems, DeVoto went on record in July 1950 in determined opposition to the Echo Dam project, first in two "Easy Chair" columns and, more prominently, in the *Saturday Evening Post,* which had a circulation of more than four million. "Shall We Let Them Ruin Our National Parks?" was widely read and stirred nationwide interest in park preservation when a condensed version appeared in the November issue of *Reader's Digest.* The article, which was DeVoto's first and last appearance in the pages of the *Post,* opened the conservationist assault on the Army Corps of Engineers and the Bureau of Reclamation as the two most dangerous enemies of parks and forests in the country. The article also laid solid foundations for the case that conservationists would build five years later against the Echo Park Dam.

The legal case against the dam was simple but compelling. By the terms of the initial National Park Act of 1916 the parks were to be set aside in perpetuity for what was termed "use without impairment." The only question was whether constructing huge

Steamboat Rock sits at the juncture of the Green and Yampa Rivers in the middle of Echo Park, which landscape architects have described as "geologically and scenically . . . the most extraordinary feature" of Dinosaur National Monument. When the Bureau of Reclamation proposed building a dam that would have obliterated the rock and its surrounding shoreline, Wallace Stegner and David Brower led a successful fight in 1955–1956 to save it. (COURTESY DINOSAUR NATURE ASSOCIATION.)

dams inside them constituted an impairment. Neither the Army Corps of Engineers nor the Reclamation Bureau thought that they did, and both agencies had on their separate drawing boards plans for dams inside Glacier National Park, Yellowstone, and Grand Canyon as well as Dinosaur. DeVoto and the conservationists knew full well that Dinosaur was intended to set a precedent. If the Reclamation Bureau could build there, it could build anywhere. As Wallace Stegner later pointed out in explaining the crucial importance of his friend's charges, "Once the protection of the National Park Act was proved ineffective, the parks would be exposed to flooding wherever one of the dam-building bureaus found a canyon it wanted to plug and a local citizenry that was interested in a boondoggle." DeVoto was determined to prevent that eventuality.

In his article for the *Saturday Evening Post* DeVoto applied the two techniques he had combined so successfully over the years— hard facts and heavy sarcasm. His facts showed that the cost-benefit figures presented by the Reclamation Bureau were in fact badly skewed and thus wholly unreliable. Nor was it at all clear that the dams inside Dinosaur and elsewhere in national parks would provide anything like the amount of water Westerners anticipated. When he shifted his attention from faulty statistics to the specific case of Echo Park, he brought his carefully honed talent for ridicule into play. If the Reclamation Bureau was able to slide its proposal for a dam at Echo Park through an inattentive Congress, he predicted, the next step would be to build a whole network of "fine highways" along the reservoirs it would create.

Then anyone who travels the 2000 miles from New York City— or 1200 from Galveston or 1000 from Seattle—will no doubt enjoy driving along these roads. He can also do still-water fishing where, before the bureau took benevolent thought of him, he could only do white-water fishing, and he can go boating or sailing on the reservoirs that have obliterated the scenery. . . . The only reason why anyone would ever go to Dinosaur National Monument is to see what the Bureau of Reclamation proposes to destroy.

The reaction to his outburst was all that DeVoto could have hoped for—howls of outrage from out of the Mountain West and votes of profound thanks from suddenly activated conservationists. An editor in Salt Lake City denounced the article as "foully misleading," and the Denver *Post* declared that what the Westerner did with his own land and water was nobody's business but his own. "The National parks happen not to be *your* scenery," DeVoto shot back. "They are *our* scenery," and "us" included the "miserable unfortunates who have to live east of the Allegheny hillocks." He added a personal admonition to the *Post* editorial writer: "Podner, as one Westerner to another, let me give you a small piece of advice before you start shooting again. Don't snoot those unfortunates too loudly or obnoxiously. You might make them so mad that they would stop paying for your water development."

By 1953 DeVoto had two years to live. At the height of his involvement with conservation issues his health began to fail. Increasingly he suffered from eyestrain, migraines, sleeplessness, and general debility. By his own admission he had always been something of a hypochondriac, constantly worrying about his numerous ailments, some of them imaginary. He had also consulted psychiatrists regularly, a routine that became a source of extreme irritation to him when others learned of it and a cause of lasting enmity when Robert Frost publicized it. Still, he managed to finish the magisterial third volume of his trilogy, *The Course of Empire,* in 1951, and Houghton Mifflin published it two years later.

Most of his time and energy thereafter was devoted to conservation matters, in particular the continuing efforts of the stockmen to privatize the national forests. Yet money was a constant worry with a lowered earning power and a high standard of Cambridge living—spacious house, frequent entertainment, a private secretary, and two boys in private school. He was now more and more dependent on articles he sent to his agent, Carol Brandt, for distribution to unresponsive editors. He refused to write on speculation—that is, with no assurance that his manuscript would be bought— and worried over his inability to secure attractive assignments. "What about it, Carol?" he asked his agent. "I can't write for magazines like the *American.* . . . The *Post* isn't much interested. What's your honest opinion? . . . Are there enough places and chances for the kind of stuff I write to make it sensible to try, or should I stick to books? Don't spare my feelings." His friends at *Harper's* scarcely improved his self-confidence by urging him to return to his old ways by broadening the range of his interests beyond what seemed to them a nearly obsessive concern with environmental issues. Advice duly noted and rejected. Through recurring bouts of depression and feelings of insecurity he kept hammering away at his adversaries old and new. As Wallace Stegner later commented in his biography of his friend, "Demoralized or not, gloomy or not, DeVoto never stopped fighting what he hated." Out of the twenty-three "Easy Chair" pieces left to him before his death in 1955 thirteen dealt with environmental problems or the crisis in civil liberties.

DeVoto's depression had both personal and political roots. It was difficult for liberal intellectuals in the McCarthy years and the accompanying Republican rollback to find much to cheer about. Stegner recalled that the completion of *The Course of Empire* and its success brought the author no real joy. There was no satisfaction equivalent to that following the publication of *The Year of Decision* a decade earlier. "All the exhilaration that American institutions had always stimulated in him was gone; his robust confidence in the country and the system had weakened, along with the depletion of his energies and the decline of his health." Nevertheless, he pushed ahead with his draft of a history of the recent West which he would not live to complete. Readers of his *Harper's* "Easy Chair" columns undoubtedly received a foretaste of DeVoto's opinions in the several accounts of the ongoing degradation of Western land and the loss of a public will. His views were as strong as ever, but they were expressed now in a language of deepening gloom.

The Republican Party and administration bore the brunt of DeVoto's sallies following the election of 1952. He accused it of ignoring its conservationist heritage, which he traced back to John Wesley Powell, Charles Sargent, Nathaniel Shaler, Carl Schurz, Othniel Marsh, WJ McGee, and Gifford Pinchot—Republicans all. It was true that all of them in their day had been forced to battle against the greed and corruption of the spoilsmen in their party, but a list of their legislative achievements summarized for the present generation of Republicans the nature of the legacy bequeathed them: the Reclamation Act, the Withdrawal Act, the Carey Act and the Weeks Act, together with Republican measures establishing institutions like the Inland Waterways Commission. The Democrat Franklin Roosevelt was only one of the three great names in conservation history; the other two—Theodore Roosevelt and Gifford Pinchot—were Republicans. Here was the true legacy of Lincoln's Republicanism. DeVoto paused at this point to remind readers that all these party heroes had been devout nationalists who had emerged from the Civil War in person or in memory with a strong sense of a national community and who had fought the particularist elements in the Democratic Party much as the Union had confronted the Confederacy. Now that political alignment had been reversed, and Republicans were attempting to revive a fraudulent and discredited states rights doctrine to help greedy private interests waste and deplete the nation's resources. Turning resource management over to the states would invite disaster, DeVoto was convinced. "It would cost the states a huge fortune—the billion-dollar jackpot in attempting to manage everything which is now taken care of by the federal government." States would have to maintain their parks with their own money. They would be forced to build their own roads, raise their own taxes for forest fire prevention and erosion control, build their own power projects, manage their own reclamation. Of course, DeVoto added sarcastically, there were other possible solutions. "The gold that is supposed to be 'locked up' in Yellowstone Park could be sold, though only at a trivial price, for trying to find it would be a highly speculative enterprise. The timber in the parks could be sold, and such scenery as might survive the construction of mining, dredging, and irrigation works could be sold to resort corporations." So go ahead! he urged the states, try it and see what happens.

It was not simply the politicians who exasperated DeVoto but the lobbyists and the special interest hacks across the country who bombarded Congress and the public with their bald falsifications of the historical record in order to further their own selfish interests. Thus when a National Chamber of Commerce spokesman recalled happier times when the public domain was there "to give every man a chance to earn land for himself through his own skill and hard work," DeVoto guffawed. Oh my yes! That sturdy corporate homesteader. Let's consult the real record. How about the Timber and Stone Act which sold 160 acres of redwood forest to a supposed "homesteader" who promptly went down to the local land office and turned his claim over to the lumber company for $50? "Under this act four million acres of publicly owned timber passed into corporate ownership at a small fraction of its value." Or consider the thousands of claims filed fraudulently with "proof" that water had been seen on the property albeit in a glass or that a "habitable dwelling" had been built—16-by-16 measured in inches rather than feet. Or the bonanza provided lumber combines, who had no need for a ruse. "They could pay a location fee, say $16 per 320 acres, and the company could forthwith clear-cut the timber and let the claim lapse."

All of these Gilded Age shenanigans, DeVoto pointed out in correcting the record, were "typical, routine, second-magnitude land frauds" nevertheless representing "the shabbiest chapter in our history." The reason why present-day land reserves had to be set aside was that unchecked monopolization of the public domain threatened to saddle the entire West with a system of peonage. Now at midcentury infinitely more powerful and vocal corporate interests, enriched by the war, were playing the same game, once again with the support of a Republican majority. The present raid on resources centered on the oil reserves underneath the marginal seas in Texas, Louisiana, and California, resources properly belonging to the public. A similar assault was being launched against public power and electric cooperatives in the name of profits. "A business administration means business, doesn't it? Prolonging federal protection of this public interest would be bureaucratic tyranny and inefficiency, wouldn't it? There is so big a melon to be cut that not to cut it would be creeping socialism—let's go."

Those sound business principles, DeVoto noted caustically but presciently, go to enrich *corporate* America, not the much-vaunted little man. "The great stands of timber will go to Big Lumber, oil and shale oil to Big Oil, minerals and chemicals to Big Mining, public power plants and sites for future ones to Big Power." The land-grabbers of the Gilded Age were small fry measured by the standards of their descendants. Yet however accurate the corporate predators' script, their casting was all wrong, for they envisioned a docile public and a compliant Congress, and in fact they could count on neither. Such was DeVoto's hope as late as 1953. Just a year later, as he weighed the comparative strength of the forces vying for control of American resources, he had become profoundly pessimistic. All of the dire predictions embedded in his twenty-year jeremiad were coming true. "Conservation: Down and on the Way Out," which appeared in the August 1954 issue of *Harper's*, rendered his final verdict.

DeVoto could have called "Conservation Down and on the Way Out" his swan song. The essay offered an extraordinarily bleak assessment of the fifties political situation and the prospects for the conservation movement. The Eisenhower administration, it appeared to him, was a business administration pure and simple without a genuine program of its own save an offer to return to the days of swindle and grab handed it by the electric power industry. Working together, the power companies and the administration had devised a formula removing the federal government from regulation of the economy. Where private enterprise can operate at a profit, kick government out. Where it cannot, force government to provide subsidies, tax relief, and pump priming. Be sure to emphasize "decentralization" as the key to local development. Open the door of the back room to the local "boys"—the chambers of commerce, trade associations, lobbies, and special interests. In short, turn the clock back to the

Gilded Age and the spoilsmen. So-called "reorganization," DeVoto scoffed, was a stab in the back to efficient regional organizations like the Park Service, the Forest Service, and the Soil Conservation Service, all of which had long perfected successful programs of regional management. The "boys" have now taken over Secretary of the Interior McKay's treasure chest, and "the predicted giveaways are in progress" while the secretary denounces conservationist opponents of the Echo Dam project as a bunch of "punks."

Meanwhile, it seemed to him as he looked about him that the conservation agencies themselves were in disarray, their nerve, energy, and imagination at a low ebb. Meanwhile, too, the Eisenhower administration wars against the electric cooperatives and community-owned distribution groups. Excluding a local cooperative owned and run by farmers in Hells Canyon, Idaho, the Department of Interior relinquishes control to the banker-directed Idaho Power Company chartered in Maine on the grounds that it is "local" whereas the farmers cooperative is not. "The company," DeVoto snorted, "is no more local enterprise than Western Union or the New York Central."

DeVoto closed the books on his grim accounting with a last look at Echo Park and the Dinosaur National Monument. The government's plan for the dam, he insisted once more, "breaches the basic national parks policy." Moreover, "the dam will destroy the beauty of the spectacular canyons of the Yampa and Green Rivers." The project was simply the most egregious attempt on the part of the administration to carve away the national commons—whether grazing lands, forests, cooperatives, parks, or principle. Using the old dodge that local people needed to be protected from Washington, national corporate interests had completely triumphed.

In a year and a half the businessmen in office have reversed the conservation policy by which the United States has been working for more than seventy years to substitute wise use of its natural resources in place of reckless destruction for the profit of special corporate interests. They have reversed most of the policy, weakened all of it, opened the ways to complete destruction. Every move in regard to conservation that the Administration has made has been against the public interest—which is to say against the future—and in favor of some special private interest. Most notably, too, every one has been in favor of some big special interest and against local small ones. The friendly partnership with business has turned out to mean only some kinds of businesses, the bigger the better.

In the meantime the American future remains caught between these destructive forces and the indisputable facts of environmental degradation. Rivers continue to fill up with silt, the water table continues to drop. Waters run off and the land dries up. Two dust bowls have formed already, and, as the adage goes, the best place now to get a Colorado farm is in eastern Kansas. "And the best place to get anything else you may want is the Department of Interior."

Wallace Stegner closed his biographical tribute to his old friend with a detailed account of the dismal year leading up to DeVoto's death in late 1955. It was not all darkness: his agent was now securing him regular assignments, and he continued to write acerbic pieces on the environment like the one lamenting tourism in Maine as turning its beaches and seaside villages into a "jerrybuilt, neon-lighted, overpopulated slum." No apparent loss of the old fire yet. But he complained regularly now about an "empty soreness or sore emptiness" in his gut and worried about hypertension even after consulting doctors who assured him that he was basically sound and that hypochondria probably explained his heightened anxiety. And he was reaping rewards and winning recognition: the National Book Award for *The Course of Empire*, yet another collection of "Easy Chair" essays, tributes from the editors of *Harper's* for twenty years of distinguished service, a scheduled appearance on national TV. It was this occasion that brought him reluctantly to New York to serve as a commentator and interpreter of the West on CBS's *Adventure* series. He could barely bring himself to go, complaining once more, "either my gut or my neurosis has been giving me hell all fall, and is giving me particularly hell now." But forcing himself one last time, he appeared on the program in the afternoon of November 13, walked to his hotel and returned to his room with his friend and doctor, Herbert Scheinberg, suffered a massive heart attack, and died in Presbyterian Hospital that evening. In preparing for the planned presentation ceremony celebrating his 241st "Easy Chair" essay he had written out a response. In it he admitted to making strong judgments all his life, some of which closed the matter right there. "But there are also judgments that require you to commit yourself, to stick your neck out. Expressing them in print obliges you to go on to advocacy." Intended, as Stegner said, as a gracious response to a well-earned tribute, his remark served even more poignantly as an obituary.

II ⌐

Bernard DeVoto died convinced that conservation as he knew it had been imprisoned inside an "Iron Triangle" made up of a powerful Western congressional bloc, influential federal agencies eager for rapid development, and clamorous local interests.

Working together they constituted a formidable enemy intent on making decisions on the basis of short-term regional interests at the expense of long-term national efficiency. Yet already in 1955, the year of his death, there were signs of stirring within the ranks of the environmentalists now finally aware of the dangers to wilderness, parks, and forests posed by unchecked development, and informed, moreover, by a new if still faint ecological awareness. For these and for the renewal of reform energy that accompanied them they had DeVoto to thank.

In crediting DeVoto with converting him to environmental activism Wallace Stegner later explained that his old friend had been "very persuasive." "He knew a lot," Stegner recalled, and had chased him "with a cattle prod" because De Voto regarded him as "a kind of protégé" in need of constant goading. Stegner also knew that for several years following World War II DeVoto had fought "almost single-handedly" fending off the grazing interests and their schemes for a gigantic landgrab. Conservationists, like Stegner himself, who were beginning to organize in earnest by the mid-fifties owed DeVoto a debt. He had not lived to see the results of his years of preaching or to learn of his success in supplying environmentalism with a pointed ethical message. Yet with it the environmental movement in 1955 was gathering a public force that would sustain it for a quarter of a century by changing the outlook on their land of millions of Americans.

When Stegner joined the Sierra Club's campaign against the Bureau of Land Reclamation's plan to build dams inside Dinosaur National Monument, he was hardly a neophyte. In his fiction and nonfiction alike, in essays and articles, in his career choice and lifestyle, Stegner had always insisted on staying "as close to earth and human experience as possible," adding that "the only earth I know is one I have lived on, the only human experience I am at all sure of is my own." He had lived at times on Utah's Plateau Province and was well aware of its need for protection. Thus when David Brower, the newly appointed executive director of the Sierra Club, approached him in 1954 and asked him to edit and contribute to a set of essays on Dinosaur National Monument, he agreed and quickly took charge of the project.

In the fifties when the energetic and confrontational David Brower took the helm, the Sierra Club was the sturdy veteran of the American conservation movement, its pedigree running back to its founding in 1892 by John Muir and friends of Yosemite. The Sierra Club, together with the National Audubon Society (1903), the National Parks and Conservation Association (1919), the Izaak Walton League (1921), the National Wildlife Association, and the Wilderness Society, formed the core of the so-called "first genera-tion" organizations concerned with wilderness and wildlife protection. All of these groups entered the second half of the twen-tieth century with limited accomplishments and distinct liabilities. Membership in all of them remained small, and they were widely viewed as elitist—as wealthy Californian backpackers in the case of the Sierra Club, as matronly Fifth Avenue bird-watchers in that of the Audubon Society. Some of them were primarily regional in outlook and program. Others, like the National Wildlife Federa-tion, as its title indicated, were leagues of state societies. All of them were almost exclusively concerned with wilderness and wildlife inside national parks and forests, and they tended to focus on particular sites in need of immediate protection.

Preserving public land from infringement by government agen-cies and private interests had not seemed all that necessary in the Depression years; economic recovery and resource development were prime considerations then. World War II and the economic boom that outlasted it changed the situation dramatically. Giant war industries sprang up together with nationally based corporations, neither of them particularly concerned with the land they occupied or the effects they produced. An unintended effect of rapid economic growth was to divide conservationists into two camps, one which continued to adhere to the principle of wise use and sensible private development, the other increasingly determined on stricter measures barring all resource development on public land. The appearance of Howard Zahniser as the charismatic new leader of the Wilderness Society in the late forties, and the appointment a few years later of David Brower as executive director of the Sierra Club marked a philosophical and political parting of the ways between older conservationists and younger preservationists. With the changing of the guard came new sets of instructions from headquarters: organize, publicize, advertise, lobby, and legislate. Which is precisely what David Brower had in mind when he approached Wallace Stegner in 1954 with a request that seemed more of a demand for a skillful piece of propaganda with which to influence votes in Congress and the views of the American public on the issue of dam building inside Dinosaur National Monument.

David Brower was a skilled mountaineer with thirty-three climbs in the Sierras to his credit. He had served on the Sierra Club's editorial board since 1935 and as its chief editor since 1946. He brought to wilderness preservation a backpacker's philosophy of total commitment, which frequently clashed with the views of his more conservative board. "Who," he asked, "once having enjoyed it, does not long for the deep satisfaction of beholding a panorama from a vantage-point, access to which has cost something in effort and training?" Brower also brought with him a strong dislike for wilderness road building, upscale campsites, and other amenities designed to attract hordes of tourists. He distrusted the

Park Service for its timidity, disliked the Forest Service as the agent of the grazing and timber interests, and held the Bureau of Land Reclamation in contempt. A refusal to consider compromise until the eleventh hour became a distinguishing mark of his style of leadership. Another was his recognition of the need for more money and improved public relations. "We could do enormously more with wilderness outings, publications, and films than we have done, and almost all the rest of the program could be carried as a result," he told his board. The most visible aspect of Brower's program was a well-honed adversarial temperament that allowed him to criticize, complain, and, if need be, impugn the motives of his opponents. These tendencies and Brower's determination to join the public relations battle against the special interests would cost the Sierra Club its tax-exempt status.

Initially Stegner was reluctant to take on Brower's assignment. He hated to give up valuable writing time on his other projects, and he was not sure that he could accept the confrontational strategy Brower had in mind. The well-known publisher, Alfred A. Knopf, who agreed to publish the collection of essays and contribute one himself, considered Brower altogether too "bossy." Stegner, for his part, realized that in terms of style and mode of operation DeVoto's mantle had fallen not on himself but on the contentious, hard-hitting Brower. As he later explained, "I'm certainly not Benny DeVoto. I haven't the capacity or the temperament to do what he did. I likewise don't have the format he did: the "Easy Chair" was a very good pulpit. He was a known personality in that place, and a lot of people read him religiously, and what he said had great effect. I can't do that, but I can at least publish articles and make some speeches. I can toss my pebbles into what I wish were an avalanche of protest." With *This Is Dinosaur* Stegner did better than that: if not exactly a boulder, the collection of essays was a good-size rock heaved at the scheme of the developmentalists.

After a heated discussion of tone and style Stegner, Brower, and Knopf agreed on the format for a set of descriptive essays on the critical importance of Dinosaur National Monument for all Americans—river rafters, scientists, historians, tourists, and nature lovers. Considering the fact that the book was completed in a three-month span, it was a superlative achievement. Eliot Blackwelder gave an account of the geological formation of the monument with a special emphasis on the juncture of the Green and Yampa Rivers at Echo Park. The veteran preservationist Olaus Murie with Joseph W. Penfold described its natural history, and the anthropologist Robert Lister told the story of its aboriginal people, their petroglyphs and artifacts. Otis "Dock" Marston provided a capsule history of successive expeditions down the rivers, from Ashley's in 1828 to Major Powell's in 1869 to those of Nathaniel Galloway in the twentieth century. The proposed dams, Marston warned, would do more than drown the parks, foreshorten cliffs, and erase archeological remains. "They would also eliminate every rapid on both the Yampa and the Green, from Lily Park and Brown's Park to the mouth of Split Mountain. In their place would be a long still-water reservoir with mud banks." In his turn David Bradley took readers careening through the Gates of Lodore and the "boom rapids" at Split Mountain before asking them whether these canyon rivers were really "worth more as kilowatts." In the concluding essay Alfred Knopf extended an open invitation to tourists and sightseers while praising park personnel for their efficiency and dedication.

Arranged in dramatic sequence throughout the collection were striking color and black-and-white photographs and drawings, nearly three dozen in all, of deep canyons and sandstone parks, cliffs, faults, rock strata, and quarries together with Dinosaur's wild inhabitants—bighorns, cougars, mule deer, and pronghorns. If Stegner intended to whet the reader's appetite for the sublime, he succeeded beyond all expectation. *This Is Dinosaur* served as a prototype of the Sierra Club's immensely popular series of illustrated books that provided the American public with visual journeys through the nation's wild places.

Stegner's lead essay, "The Marks of Human Passage," united his political philosophy with an acute sense of felt history. His philosophy of moderation, which would continue to determine his actions and outlook as it had in the past, was later summed up in an interview. "There are among environmentalists a sentimental fringe, people who respond . . . with blind preservationism in all circumstances," he explained. He quickly added, "But you can't do that. You manifestly can't go that far, though it would be nice, visually and in other ways; people do have to live too. Some kind of compromise has to be made." This was the spirit in which he undertook his own history of Dinosaur, its early inhabitants and later visitors.

Stegner opened his essay with a definition of wilderness that may have startled strict preservationists. Dinosaur Monument, he told them, was "almost unspoiled" and only "relatively unmarked." The best way to visualize the three-pronged area with its two rivers was to see it as "a palimpsest of human history, speculation, rumor, fantasy, ambition, science, controversy, and conflicting plans for use." He briefly described the topography and rehearsed the geological history of Dinosaur before reminding readers that it was not simply these physical facts that defined it but "the marks" human beings have put on it. To understand the real meaning of the land we have to begin with its human history and the signs that its various peoples left behind them. First the Anasazi who flourished between 400 and 800 A.D. Theirs were literally marks—pictographs and petroglyphs chipped into the faces of cliffs, handprints and footprints pressed on flat rocks. Together with granaries in the caves and ancient campsites on the terraces, these were the earliest signs of habitation.

It was nearly a thousand years before the next mark appeared, this one made by outsiders on their way through the desert to California. In 1776, as British colonists along the Atlantic seaboard rebelled against their mother country, the Spanish explorer Don Joaquin Lain camped along the Green on his way from New Mexico to Monterey and carved his name and the date in a huge black cottonwood on its bank, an act duly noted by Fray Silvestre Veléz de Escalante in his diary entry for September 14 of that year.

The next mark was made some forty-nine years later by General William Henry Ashley and his six mountain men who took the water route in bullboats through Desolation Canyon in their search for a pathway to the south. "Ashley, 1825" was the general's reminder painted on a rock but left unidentified for nearly a century when Ashley's journal was finally published in 1918. Ashley in turn was followed by bullwhackers on a forty-niner wagon train who foolishly attempted Disaster Falls in Lodore until dissuaded from going further by a Ute chief who advised them to head overland to Salt Lake City. "So," Stegner comments, "except for the healed or rotted inscription in the cottonwood on its southern boundary, and the name of Ashley just outside its northern prong, Dinosaur had no recorded white history until past the middle of the nineteenth century."

The next visitor to Dinosaur country, however, was a man with a different purpose—Major John Wesley Powell, who came with a desire to study the country and get to know its Native American inhabitants. Powell passed Ashley's daub in 1869 and misread the

William Bell, *Utah Series No. 10: Hieroglyphic Pass, Opposite Parowan*, Utah (1872). Bell, a photographer from Philadelphia, accompanied one of the many western surveys conducted in the 1870s and recorded what Stegner eighty years later would call "the marks of human passage" across the Plateau Province.

date before moving on down river. It was Powell, as Stegner had explained in his biography, who was the real discoverer of the Dinosaur canyons because "he brought knowledge to them" and at the same time learned from its residents, whose languages he studied and whose customs he diligently recorded.

It was not Major Powell who was responsible for preserving Dinosaur, however, but a dedicated field geologist and paleontologist named Lewis Douglass whose story Stegner had told briefly in *Mormon Country*. Douglass discovered his dinosaur deposit in 1909 when he stumbled across a row of brontosaur vertebrae just below Split Mountain Canyon. Douglass proceeded to spend the next fifteen years hacking, scraping, and chiseling at the rocks and removing and labeling the remains he uncovered before shipping them off to the Carnegie Museum's Hall of Vertebrate Paleontology in Pittsburgh—some 700,000 pounds of them eventually. To protect his find from souvenir hunters he enlisted the Carnegie Museum, which obliged by successfully urging President Woodrow Wilson in 1915 to declare Douglass's site and a surrounding eight acres a national monument. FDR enlarged the acreage in 1938, making a 325-square-mile preserve to protect endangered watersheds. There it now stands, declared Stegner, "sanctuary from a world paved with concrete, jet-propelled, smog-bracketed, sterilized, over-insured, aseptic, a world mass-produced with interchangeable parts, and with every natural beautiful thing endangered by the raw engineering power of the twentieth century."

Stegner's capsule history served as prologue to his closing message of moderate use, a philosophy linking people and place in symbiotic relation. "A place is nothing in itself," he reminded his readers. "It has no meaning, it can hardly be said to exist, except in terms of human perception, use, and response. . . . We cannot even describe a place except in terms of its human uses." Some of these uses use things up, but others can be made to last forever. Recreation, properly managed, could be a perpetual use "and a vital one." He closed his appeal with a quote from an old river rat named Pat Lynch, who left a note in his riverside cave in 1886 for his visitors:

> If in those caverns you shelter take
> Plais do them no harm
> Lave everything you find around hanging up or on the ground

Pat Lynch's request, Stegner commented, contained the real meaning of the collection of essays: use but don't harm.

By the time Stegner undertook the rush job of editing *This Is Dinosaur* David Brower had carried the fight to Washington, where both House and Senate Subcommittees on Irrigation and Reclamation were holding hearings on the Colorado River Storage Project. Brower's strategy was twofold. He provided a powerful visual argument with striking photographs of the famous Hetch Hetchy before and after a dam was built—magnificent cliffs and lush groves reduced to grim mud banks and dead tree stumps. No need to ask the question "Do you want Echo Park to look like this?" Brower's other maneuver was to tackle head-on before the House committee the Bureau of Reclamation's case for the dam. The bureau's argument for the Echo Park site rested in large measure on seemingly irrefutable statistics showing that evaporation rates behind the dam would be much lower than at any other spot on the river. Brower surprised and then outraged the Bureau's experts and their Western supporters by challenging and then disproving their figures. Brower presented himself in the true DeVoto tradition as a simple amateur with only a layman's knowledge of mathematics, but under the pressure of hostile questioning from the floor he reversed course. "My point," he shot back at his irate questioners, "is to demonstrate to this committee that they would be making a great mistake to rely on the figures presented by the Bureau of Reclamation when they cannot add, subtract, multiply, or divide. I am not trying to sound smart, but it is an important thing." Working through the bureau's figures on a blackboard supplied him, Brower proceeded to demonstrate and then to force the bureau's experts to admit that indeed their arithmetic had been faulty and that the evaporation rates should be reduced from 165,000 acre-feet to 70,000 acre-feet. Subsequently the bureau's engineers readjusted that corrected figure to a mere 25,000 acre-feet. Which prompted Brower to ask sardonically how much lower they could go and still be wrong.

Undeterred, both subcommittees, stacked with Western congressmen, reported out favorably the Colorado River Storage Project with the Echo Park Dam left in. Their decision, however, prompted a blizzard of protest to descend on the Capitol—letters, articles, editorials, fliers and direct appeals to spare Dinosaur Monument. The result was a postponement while the Bureau of Reclamation presumably recalculated its statistics. Meanwhile Brower, Howard Zahniser of the Wilderness Society, and William Voigt of the Izaak Walton League were busy orchestrating a concerted public reaction against Echo Park Dam. Mail running ten to one against the project poured into Congress as Wallace Stegner and his contributors put the finishing touches on *This Is Dinosaur*. But the dam's supporters in the Mountain West states were also vigorously organizing, collecting money, and recruiting supporters at home and in Washington, D.C. By the beginning of 1955 they remained confident that they could carry the day for the Storage Project. For their part Brower, Stegner, and the preservationist leaders were concerned lest they be dismissed as "jest-aginners" unwilling to negotiate. By early 1955, Brower with Stegner's approval had hit on a compromise. Perhaps the day would come when the principle of preservation could stand on its own without trade-offs, he admitted, but that day was not yet. The Sierra Club's leadership, Brower announced in a booklet for members, "have been persuaded by practical men that one way to prevent invasion is to offer alternatives to that invasion." The alternative, it was quickly understood, involved the exchange of Echo Park Dam for a higher one outside the Monument at Glen Canyon. It took another year of wrangling and hair-splitting among proponents and opponents of development before the deal was struck. But in March 1956 the House and then the Senate approved a compromise solution excluding Dinosaur but allowing four main storage dams outside the Monument—Curecanti Dam on the Gunnison River, Flaming Gorge Dam on the Green, Navajo Dam on the San Juan, and Glen Canyon on the lower Colorado. The president signed the bill into law on April 14, 1956.

Stegner and Brower soon came to regret what seemed a bad if not exactly a corrupt bargain. Luna Leopold, the son of Aldo Leopold and a well-regarded hydrologist in the U.S. Geological Service, had warned that "if the Sierra Club gets into the problem of suggesting alternatives for the Echo Park and Split Mountain Dam you are going to let yourself wide open." So it had proved, as both Brower and Stegner ruefully admitted. Brower placed the responsibility directly on himself and the Sierra Club leadership. "The Sierra Club gave up," he said as he looked back on what now appeared to have been a give-away "and the opposition to the whole project thereupon collapsed. . . . The Sierra Club was the keystone in that, and the keystone was pulled out and the arch collapsed." Stegner employed a different metaphor in faulting the club for its lack of political savvy:

We really whipped the Upper Colorado River project. We could have strangled it to death. We had it down completely. They took the dams out of Dinosaur in a desperate conviction that if they didn't they were going to lose the whole thing. Maybe we should have been harder-nosed than we were, but that's hindsight. Having saved Dinosaur, we accepted the ruin of Glen Canyon, which was not very smart of us. . . . Nobody knew Glen Canyon then except me; I'd been down it a couple of times, and I told [Brower] it was better than Echo Park. He didn't believe it, and I didn't push it.

Later Stegner and Brower took a last run down the canyon before the engineers began filling it up, and they realized what they had lost. One could imagine the shade of Benny DeVoto along for the ride and slowly shaking his head in disbelief at what seemed his friend's unaccountable failure of nerve.

Once the dam in Glen Canyon had been built and Lake Powell began to drown the cliffs upriver Stegner seized a chance to make public his regret albeit in muted tones. *Holiday* magazine, whose editors earlier eviscerated DeVoto's article on the High Country, commissioned Stegner to do a nostalgic piece on Glen Canyon then and now but without overt criticism of policymakers and their mistakes. Stegner obliged but stood his ground when the editors sought to moderate his statement of loss. "Lake Powell" appeared in the May 1966 issue of *Holiday* and was later collected under the title "Glen Canyon Submersus" in *The Sound of Mountain Water*. Stegner recalled for readers rafting down the San Juan River to its juncture with the Colorado in 1947 and camping along the "stream of history" beneath a sandstone ledge and two arched caves "with clean cliffs soaring up behind and a long green sandbar across the river." Seventeen years later, fearing the worst, he returned to see for himself just how much of "a potentially superb national park" was left. He was surprised and mildly pleased to discover that Lake Powell in its own domesticated way was actually quite beautiful. "It isn't Glen Canyon," he admitted, "but it is something in itself"—a scaled-down version of the original but with deep blue water, truncated forms, and widened vistas. Up the lake from the dam some of the smaller side canyons still survived, and a few of the larger ones remained as impressive as he remembered them. The biggest surprise was Escalante Canyon, still one of "the stunning scenic experiences of a lifetime" and more accessible now by lake than it had ever been by foot or horseback.

Offsetting a certain exhilaration, however, was Stegner's "consciousness of loss" and nagging fears for the future. Pleased that the canyons and the entire river were now "democratically accessible" and reconciled, in part, to noisy power boats and hordes of water skiers, he was apprehensive lest future drawdowns or cliff drownings destroy what had managed to survive. "A mixture of losses, diminishments, occasional gains precariously maintained by a temporary stabilization of the lake" was his final verdict. Could anything be done, he wondered, to serve both tourist and wilderness lover? He found his answer to the conflicting demands of seemingly antagonistic communities after a night spent up Escalante Canyon "in a stillness like no other." Why not build a huge boom across the mouth of the canyon and require those determined to proceed to meet wilderness on its own terms? "What might have been done for Glen Canyon as a whole may still be done for the higher tributaries of the Escalante. Why not? In the name of scenery, silence, sanity, why not?"

If the election of Eisenhower and the Republican triumph in 1952 plunged DeVoto into deep despair at the dim prospects for a federally managed environmental program, Kennedy's victory eight years later raised a measure of hope in Stegner. That hope would steadily dwindle in the course of the sixties as he followed the path taken by millions of moderate liberals from initial promise to final alienation. He could not have guessed the outcome when, following Kennedy's inauguration, he was approached with a proposition by the vigorous, new Secretary of Interior, Stewart Udall, to whom he had sent a copy of *Beyond The Hundredth Meridian*. Udall, who greatly admired the book, asked its author to come to Washington and serve as his informal assistant and artist-in-residence. After a bit of soul-searching Stegner agreed to spend the last half of 1961 helping Udall whom he in turn admired for "his distaste for liquidation." With his decision Stegner entered yet another "learning period," as he later called it, but what he chiefly learned was his unsuitability for the political life. What struck him most forcibly in Washington was the agonizing slowness with which the federal government responded to the needs of its constituents and the inadequacy of that response when it finally came. Although he did not specify, he might have been referring to Howard Zahniser's sixty-six drafts of his wilderness bill submitted more than a full decade before Congress finally passed it in grievously weakened form in 1964.

For six months Stegner was an "idea man" for the determined Udall who dispatched him to Canyonlands, Escalante Basin, the Arches, and Cathedral to survey likely sites for national parks. Stegner mildly enjoyed participating in the formulation of environmental policy, but Mary was bored and lonely in Washington and was happy to return to Los Altos. Stegner's major contribution to his beleaguered boss was to advise him to escape the growing band of his Western critics by writing a book. With the aid of Stegner's outline, notes, and chapter proposals Udall produced *The*

Quiet Crisis, which was published in 1963. Provided a friendly political environment by a like-minded advocate of wilderness protection, Stegner proved to himself that he could make a contribution, however indirect, to federal policymaking. The political battles over David Brower's leadership of the Sierra Club, which greeted him on his return home, proved a different story.

Stegner was persuaded to run for the board of directors of the Sierra Club by his good friend and fellow moderate Ansel Adams, whose photography he admired as greatly as he did Robert Frost's poetry. He agreed to run, was elected, and served on the board from 1964 to 1968. The political turbulence that swept across the country in the sixties also caught up the Sierra Club in an acrimonious debate over leadership, proper direction and strategy, and the ethics of reform. And once again Stegner discovered how much he disliked rough-and-tumble politics and the unrewarding task of conciliating hostile forces. From the onset of the battle over leadership his loyalty had been divided between David Brower, whom he admired for the energy and drive with which he had reinvigorated the Sierra Club, and Ansel Adams, with whom Stegner shared the conviction that a nonconfrontational style was the only way to build a national constituency. As the disagreement over Brower's leadership grew sharper, Stegner found himself siding with Adams. Both men were masters at rendering artistic images of the landscapes of the Mountain West, one with a camera and what his friend called "austerity, even severity," the other with evocative verbal coloring. It was the artist's distaste for political bickering that made them oppose Brower's defiant protectionist stance.

The trouble first arose over Mineral King, a gorgeous mountain valley hard by Sequoia National Park. In the immediate postwar boom club members had seemingly agreed to Disney Corporation's proposal for a ski resort in the valley. Now, a decade later, younger Sierra Club members led by David Brower and a partisan follower, Martin Litton, prevailed upon the board to reconsider the earlier decision and call for a public hearing. Stegner supported this decision to reconsider despite his growing uneasiness with Brower's managerial style. He had been badly stung by the Echo Park compromise and was determined not to make the same mistake twice. Recently, he knew, Marble and Bridge Canyons had been saved from the dam builders but at the expense of a huge coal-fired generating plant at Four Corners which spewed noxious emissions for hundreds of miles around.

Stegner's break with Brower resulted from another compromise with developers, this one over the club's agreement with Pacific Gas and Electric, which relocated a nuclear plant from the Nipomo Dunes below San Luis Obispo to Diablo Canyon, a pristine site below Montana de Oro State Park. Once again the board had agreed to a swap that Brower's followers challenged in calling for a reconsideration. This time Stegner, together with Ansel Adams, voted against the demand to reconsider. Stegner's explanation of his vote, made years later, was less than convincing. Admitting that he had been disturbed by the Diablo deal, he nevertheless felt that reneging on an agreement would have been "unfortunate." "You shouldn't make deals until you're absolutely sure."

The Diablo Canyon episode precipitated a crisis that pitted the Sierra Club's board against its staff over the question of who held the power. Stegner confessed to not understanding any of the details even while admitting that "you had to take your choice." He chose to block Brower's bid for total control. Brower, he recalled, "was taking the club on a confrontationalist course which probably was not the most productive course it could take. . . . He was on the right side, we all agree; it was just a question of tactics. . . . I didn't, I guess, agree with Dave on the confrontation business, because it didn't seem to me to be productive." Brower's belated attempt to enlist Stegner on his side without consulting him beforehand tipped the balance. Stegner, irritated at such presumption, accused him publicly of having been bitten "by some worm of power" and voted against his slate in the election that ousted him as executive director in 1969.

Stegner may have hoped to escape political wrangling by retiring from the Sierra Club's board of directors in 1968 and returning to Stanford and teaching, but he was soon grievously disillusioned. By the late sixties the Stanford campus, like that at nearby Berkeley and colleges and universities across the country, was seething with student protest against the Vietnam War and those academic institutions that refused to take a stand opposing it. Ed McClanahan, a Stegner Fellow with whose flamboyant radicalism Stegner was "not thrilled," recalled the campus uproar as "what we might call, in retrospect, the General All-Purpose Up-Yours Movement." When campus demonstrations grew violent, as they soon did at Stanford and elsewhere, Stegner became furious at what he regarded as the arrogant self-indulgence of the protesters. He had opposed the war from the beginning and had taken an early part in protesting against it peacefully, but the smug moralism of the students made the prospect of teaching them less and less inviting. The younger generation's contempt for the past was forcibly brought home to him by an uncomprehending student's innocent question after reading *Wolf Willow*. "Why do you care where you came from?" she asked. "Isn't it what you *are* that matters?" "Now," he commented, although not to his questioner, "is a big word with the young, almost as big a word as wow." His remembered West was being "dissolved in strobe lights to the pounding of folk rock," and the achievement of a founding generation had become "a thing to smile at." He countered with a claim for the indispensability of the historical imagination. "But if you are any part of an artist, and a lot of people are some part of one, if you have any desire to understand and thus help steer a civilization that seems to have gotten away from us, then I think you don't choose between the past and the present; you try to find the connections, you try to make one serve the other."

With *The Gathering of Zion*, published in 1964, Stegner supplied his own example of the personal need for history. His account of the pioneer Mormon exodus to Utah, subtitled *The Story of the Mormon Trail*, was written for McGraw-Hill's American Trail Series in the hope of healthy sales and royalties. The appeal of the subject was particularly strong, for here was a chance to tell a different story of a great migration from the one DeVoto had recounted in *The Year of Decision: 1846.* If DeVoto's was a tale of initiation, the Mormon story was one of vindication. The Gentiles traveling the Oregon Trail or the California Trail were only passing through the Mountain West. The Mormons intended to stay and build the celestial city. Just here lay the opportunity to forge connecting links between a mythologized Mormon past and the living world of Stegner's young manhood in Salt Lake City. The original gathering and its sequences had directly impinged on his own life, and telling the story invited self-discovery.

Early on in the process of writing and again in an afterword Stegner felt the need to establish his interpretive position as a historian confronting a sensitive subject. "I write as a non-Mormon but not as a Mormon-hater," he stated candidly. Except as their strong religious faith strengthened the emigrants' will to succeed, he intentionally ignored it. "I do not believe it, but I do not quarrel with it either." He accepted the Church's organizational principles but remained "suspicious" of the hierarchy "in a way I am suspicious of any large and very powerful commercial and industrial corporation." Such an open-minded and evenhanded approach did not recommend him to the Church historian who refused to make the archives available to him. Official rejection failed to slow Stegner's research because he realized that in any case the historian was necessarily an interloper. Salt Lake City was the place "where part of my heart is," and the part of Western history that seemed most personal and real to him was Mormon history. "Nevertheless," he insisted, "I write as an outsider."

As an outside investigator he pored over the hundreds of pages of Mormon diaries, journals, and reminiscences that were made available to him and uncovered the predictable mixture of the admirable and the deplorable. "Suffering, endurance, discipline, faith, brotherly and sisterly charity, the qualities so thoroughly celebrated by Mormon writers, were surely well distributed among them, but theirs was a normal amount of human cussedness, vengefulness, masochism, backbiting, violence, ignorance, selfishness, and gullibility." It was this odd combination of heroism and intransigence that challenged the role that Stegner had decided to play in reconstructing but also evaluating and judging people and events.

Stegner's saga of the Mormon exodus is divided into two acts—the first "gathering" the escape from Nauvoo, Illinois, after Joseph Smith was murdered by a mob of non-Mormons, together with the subsequent treks of the American faithful; the second the heartrending accounts of the nearly insurmountable difficulties encountered by impoverished and ill-equipped English converts, which climaxed in the sufferings of the handcart pioneers who were caught in early winter storms en route to Salt Lake City in 1856. In both acts of his drama Stegner's presence as stage manager is constant as he arranges the experiences and reactions of his successive emigrants, many of them women, as they recorded them in their diaries and journals. "That I do not accept the faith that possessed them does not mean I doubt their frequent devotion and heroism in its service. Especially their women. Their women were incredible." Beneath the innumerable examples of personal endurance and fortitude lay the larger lesson the Mormon emigrants taught their contemporaries and later generations as "the most systematic, organized, disciplined, and successful pioneers in our history.

> Their advantage over the random individualists who preceded them and followed them up the valley of the Platte came directly from their 'un-American' social and religious organization. Where Oregon emigrants and argonauts bound for the gold fields lost practically all their social cohesion en route, the Mormons moved like the Host of Israel they thought themselves. Far from loosening their social organization, the trail perfected it. As communities on the march they proved extraordinarily adaptable. . . . When their villages on wheels reached the valley of their destination, the Saints were able to revert at once, because they were town-and-temple builders and because they had their families with them, to the stable agrarian life in which most of them had grown up.

No amount of carping and nitpicking by Mormon critics at Stegner's unsympathetic reading of their history could call into question his genuine admiration. The challenge for the historian, however, and proof of the need to link the past to the present lay in the problem bequeathed by the pioneers and settlers to later generations of how to combine such splendid solidarity with democratic processes and individual liberties. The indispensability of history, in other words, lay in the difficult questions it posed.

By the sixties Stegner's writing fellows program had achieved success and recognition. Soon after his arrival at Stanford he had set up a multitiered writing program for undergraduates and graduate students alike, a scheme he modified in the next few years while increasing the number of fellowships that went to nonmatriculating candidates soon designated "Stegner Fellows," who wrote and discussed their work in the workshops he ran with an unassuming authority. Stegner always made a point of emphasizing the democratic reach of his program, which remained open to all talents. From the outset the operation was distinctly cosmopolitan, attracting writers like Tillie Olsen, Wendell Berry, Ernest Gaines, and Al Young as well as more distinctly Western writers like Larry McMurtry, Thomas McGuane, and Edward Abbey. Occasional visitors included Katherine Anne Porter, C.P. Snow, Elizabeth Bowen, and Frank O'Connor. Stegner had returned west in 1946 with a regional writer's sensitivity to the slights dispensed by an Eastern literary establishment that tended to ignore writers west of Mississippi. If not an outraged regional patriot like his friend Benny DeVoto, he nevertheless remarked that the reputation of a writer tended to "wither" with the distance from the Atlantic seaboard. Only after a number of years did he accept the designation "Western writer," which initially struck him as a put-down and a dismissal.

Over the years Stegner came to realize that there indeed was such a literary animal as a Western writer even though he appeared in the quite different guises of a Walter Van Tilburg Clark, a Bud Guthrie, or a Norman Maclean. What they and many of the writers in his program had in common was a shared understanding of their region and its peoples. As he explained, they were "inheritors of the same western estate" with a strong distaste for "the profane western culture . . . and the oversimplified good guy/bad guy moralities invented mainly by East Coast dudes." What he and his fellow writers of the West were really doing was "creating a past, firming up a ground on which the present can stand and by which it can be comprehended." This conviction he brought to all his teaching.

The attack on Stegner's commitment to history came from two different though related quarters: from young rebels like the novelist Ken Kesey, a dissident member of Stegner's writing program who rejected the past as the source of an entrenched and repressive authority; and from those who, like the poet Gary Snyder, sought to transcend history in moments of meditation. Against Kesey's diatribes Stegner stood on the defensive, fending off charges of stodginess and irrelevance and countering Kesey's demands for the totally free spirit. Against the "hippie poet," as he persisted in calling Snyder, Stegner argued passionately the inadequacies of Buddhist mysticism as a cure for Christian insistence on subduing the wilderness. Of his two opponents, Kesey caused him the most grief, irritation, and eventual anger, which he only partially assuaged by creating his fictional counterpart in Jim Peck in *All the Little Live Things* (1967). With Snyder he was somewhat more generous after discovering that they shared a similar love of wilderness, but he could never muster much enthusiasm for the poet's work. "Maybe it's the Zen business," he explained some years later to Richard Etulain, a young friend and interviewer, "that keeps me from fully appreciating him," as he recalled a younger Snyder's offhand remark that all human achievement could be reproduced by meditation. "Damn it, I don't think that's a very sensible statement."

Stegner supplied a quiet critical intelligence in managing his program and advising its participants. "Wally was very businesslike," Al Young remembered. "He would tell you exactly what he thought, and he would be considerate of your feelings, but he would not pull his punches. He had a manner, a style, that was gentle. And he would give you bad news in a gentle way." Bad news, no matter how gently delivered, was not what Ken Kesey had in mind for his own work. Talented, imaginative, assertive, and seemingly cocksure, Kesey, like many untried writers, was also wary, protective, and thin-skinned, unable to accept criticism with good grace. For his part, Stegner detected an exaggeration and a certain phoniness in Kesey's noisy celebration of nonconformity. Kesey in turn resented comments that struck him as all too moderate and judicious, suggestions that smacked of Victorian verities and stylistic reserve. Increasingly his responses gave vent to a patricidal urge deep inside him. He told friends and admirers of Stegner's work that the master's best years were long behind him and that he wrote chiefly now "to a classroom and his colleagues." To Kesey his would-be mentor seemed the embodiment of bankrupt authority. Asked what he had learned from Stegner, he shot back: "Just never to teach in college." And what of Stegner's influence on his work? Wholly negative. "I have felt impelled into the future by Wally, by his dislike of what I was doing, what we were doing. This was the kiss of approval in some way."

Here Kesey touched on the fundamental philosophical difference between teacher and student, the older man's deepening conservative estimate of the possibility of drastic change and the younger's fierce determination to forge ahead, smash tradition, and leave a discredited power structure in shambles. Disagreements on style and craft were thus grounded in markedly different Wests. Stegner accused Kesey of trying to breathe new life into a moribund mythical hero, the lone horseman dear to moviegoers but unknown to history—valiant and virtuous to a fault but unreflecting and ultimately irresponsible. Kesey's invented hero McMurphy in *One Flew Over the Cuckoo's Nest* was Hollywood's mythic cowpuncher run to seed, fit now only for a fatal walkdown with Big Nurse. Stegner's chief objection to such fantasizing, aside from its self-indulgence, was its blinding sentimentality that obscured the shaping force of the past on the present. Lacking a sense of history, the younger generation, following Kesey's advice, seemed doomed to inhabit an "amputated present" cut off from any knowledge of a "personal and *possessed* past." To illustrate he abandoned his old pontoon bridge metaphor for the image of a lifeline. "In the old days," he wrote, "in blizzardy weather, we used to tie a string of lariats from house to barn so as to make it from shelter to responsibility and back again. With personal, family, and cultural chores to do, I think we had better rig up such a line between past and present."

In his quarrel with Gary Snyder, Stegner went on the offensive in a heated exchange that eventually cooled into an agreement to disagree. It was a sign of Stegner's strengthened preference for moderation that he attacked Snyder in the pages of *The Nation* for his brash claim that the new revolutionaries would not leave a single old American value standing, a pronouncement that Snyder quickly disavowed while continuing to insist that "real values" had nothing to do with social orders "new or old." Stegner found this kind of arrogance hard to swallow even though he admitted in a letter of half-apology to Snyder that "we may have more in common than you think." What they shared was a consuming love of wilderness and the determination to "do no harm," advice that Stegner attributed to the river rat Pat Lynch and Snyder to Buddha. Snyder's memory of the shaping places in his life was nearly as keen as Stegner's of Eastend: "San Francisco, North Beach, like living on the bow of a ship. Over the dark running seas, from November on, breaking in rains and flying cloud bits on the sharp edges of Telegraph Hill." Yet for Stegner, Zen spelled the sufficiency of meditation, and meditation isolated the individual, preventing the true believer from taking direct constructive action.

What supplied the animus to Stegner's argument against the sixties generation was not simply its adolescent penchant for self-dramatization but an all-too-apparent willingness to live truncated lives imprisoned in the present. This misconception permeated everything the young thought or wrote. "No matter how I try, I cannot believe in the 'liberated' consciousness that is the subject of so much contemporary writing," he complained. "Though I may enjoy these productions, and may even myself play games with Kronos as a literary exercise, I want a foot on earth, I am forced to believe in Time. I believe we are Time's prisoners, I believe Time is our safety and strength." This conviction, he admitted, was particularly strong in people like himself who had grown up deprived of a history and to compensate had developed an inordinate interest in place and local lore. "The discovery that it has been around them all the time, and that they were deprived of it, shatters their ability to take it for granted as inheritors of a stabler civilization might do."

Stegner's disagreement with his students also soured his relations with his colleagues in Stanford's English Department and writing program. The sixties brought a vast cultural as well as political sea change to American academia. The shift in consciousness was multifold, involving art as well as politics in fracturing objective reality into bits of disconnected consciousness and collapsing time by emphasizing subjectivity and interiority. At Stanford the bearer of the modernist banner was Stegner's colleague Yvor Winters whose proselytizing precipitated a battle over academic turf and at a deeper level produced an ongoing debate on the philosophy and practice of art. The difference between the two men's artistic worlds was brought home to Stegner by Winters's insensitive dismissal of his favorite poet, Robert Frost, as "a poet of the minor theme, the casual approach, and the discreetly eccentric attitude." Competition between the two teachers soon became an open rivalry for recognition, students, and funds for Stegner's fellowship program and Winters's smaller poetry workshop with both men dug in defending their respective territories.

The teaching of writing in American colleges and universities in the sixties also reflected a massive shift in social and political perceptions. And nowhere was this development clearer than on the Stanford campus when a native son, Albert Guerard, returned in 1961 with new ideas for an experimental "Voice Program" for freshman composition designed to encourage spontaneity and experimentation at the expense of expository rules and rhetorical models. Guerard wanted freedom from departmental constraints and control, and his tenacity in pursuing his goal put him in direct confrontation with Stegner, for whom craft meant careful construction and frequent revision. Stegner's advice to would-be writers was direct and succinct: "You don't go out and 'commit experience' for the sake of writing about it later; and if you have to make notes on how a thing has struck you, it probably hasn't struck you."

The combination of ongoing student protest against the war and political battles inside the English department proved too much for Stegner who by 1971 decided that he had had enough. The issues converged in the person of Bruce Franklin, an enthusiastic and popular young teacher who vowed publicly to make Maoists of his students and proceeded to distribute copies of Chairman

Mao's little red book. Stegner's objections earned him a personal attack in the Stanford *Daily* and a reason to quit. "That ends it," he told his officemate. "I am not going to do anything more. I'm washing my hands of the whole business." Looking back on his decision, he admitted to feeling a real letdown. "It was not a time when teaching was any fun anymore, and why the hell didn't I get out?" Though not precisely fun, two major projects promised genuine satisfaction. *Angle of Repose*, the massive novel on which he had been working for some time, appeared in 1971, and three years later *The Uneasy Chair*, his biographical tribute to his old friend Benny DeVoto, at once a labor of undying affection and a compelling summary of their shared outlook on history and the American land.

Stegner's most powerful rejoinder to a doubting younger generation on the indispensability of history took the form of a major novel and this, his best work, *Angle of Repose*. The novel earned him a Pulitzer Prize and, ironically, the disdain of a group of professional historians who accused him of distorting the life of a real woman and plagiarizing her letters. The woman in question was Mary Hallock Foote, a talented late Victorian writer and artist who had come to the Mountain West with her husband, a mining engineer, and whose life and work vividly dramatized the cultural clash between a settled East and a frontier West. Stegner had heard of Mary Hallock Foote soon after his arrival at Stanford, but it was not until a graduate student of his gave up the idea of editing her work that he took a direct interest in her. By that time—the early sixties—other historians unknown to him were already contemplating that editing project. Thus the fictional figure of Susan Burling Ward, Stegner's name for his heroine, competed for attention and invited comparison with her real-life counterpart. When Stegner used some of Foote's letters in creating her fictional counterpart in his novel, the ensuing criticism ranged from complaints of misrepresentation to charges of plagiarism. His best novel thus became the source of his bitter disappointment.

Stegner recognized in Mary Hallock Foote a model for his story of the cultural clash, marital stress, and personal anguish involved in the uprooting of a genteel and greatly talented young woman and her transplantation in a crude and atomistic frontier West. The real life of Foote, he realized from the outset, would require altering, adjusting, and adapting—"bending" he called it—to make the story he wanted to tell of a tragically flawed marriage that neither partner had allowed to fail. Once before he had made the passage between fact and fiction in telling the story of Joe Hill. There he had invented out of whole cloth a scene in the California hopfields where the migrant worker Hill murders his boss in a fit of rage. It was this kind of falsifying of the historical record which outraged surviving members of the IWW who objected to the slandering of their martyred leader. Similarly the practitioners of the new women's history were offended by the seeming misappropriation of Mary Hallock Foote's letters to her friend back home in the East. Stegner did in fact quote freely from them—some thirty-five out of a total of five hundred—and some of them at considerable length, others with alterations. For his part, Stegner considered his admission in an introductory note to the novel thanking Foote's granddaughters a sufficient explanation and defense of his method. "Though I have used many details of their [the Foote husband and wife's] lives and characters, I have not hesitated to warp both personalities and events to fictional needs. This is a novel which utilizes selected facts from real lives. It is in no sense a family history."

The author's explanation failed to mollify Foote's descendants, one of whom was co-editing her grandmother's papers and realized the extent of Stegner's borrowing or, as she thought, stealing. For Stegner the letters were crucial in supplying the raw stuff of the family history his protagonist seeks to unravel. It is this second story of the working historian and the effect of his findings on his own life that constitutes the main interest in *Angle of Repose*. Lyman Ward is a retired professor of history who painfully reconstructs the troubled lives of his grandparents. Lyman Ward as Stegner presents him is "a narrator with a broken marriage and a broken body," a misanthrope with an amputated leg and a frozen spine, living a life of constant pain and in need of the constant care that he grudgingly accepts. In a later conversation with Richard Etulain, Stegner explained his intent in creating Lyman Ward: "He was in a box, as it seemed to me, speaking from a box rather hollowly, desperately reconstructing the life of his grandmother and desperately avoiding his own. It seemed to me that the present and the past could be brought together that way." Which is precisely what happens. As Lyman, crippled and virtually immobilized, talks into his tape recorder explaining his findings, he digresses, confesses, apologizes, and improvises. Proceeding on mere hunches and relying frequently on inference, he is, as his creator explained, "not only recorder, but he was a guesser, interpreter, and he wasn't a reliable witness." Yet Lyman is mysteriously enlarged by his investigation; he learns from the process of discovery and is changed by it to the point of at least considering a reconciliation with his estranged wife who would care for him in his infirmity. In Lyman's tentative gesture toward reunion, past and present are finally and indissolubly bound together in the mind of the historian whose recognition of that fact can liberate him from a life of isolation and loneliness. In its two interwoven stories *Angle of Repose* is an unassailable rejoinder to Stegner's undergraduate who asked him why he cared about the past.

Stegner was stunned, then hurt, and finally annoyed by the charges leveled against his book, which he, like most readers, considered his best work. He refused to see the problem. After all, he had received the family's permission to use the Foote papers and had offered to let them read the manuscript before publication, an offer they had declined. Moreover, he had written a *novel*, not a biography. "It has nothing to do with the actual life of Mary Hallock Foote except I borrowed a lot of her experiences. So I don't, I guess, feel very guilty about that. It is a method that I've used . . . to mix history and fiction. And whenever fact will serve fiction—and I am writing fiction—I am perfectly willing to use it that way." He had done no damage to Mary Hallock Foote because her papers, including the letters, were only the "raw material" out of which a novel might be made. If certain critics failed to see it that way—or to *read* it that way—that was their business, not his.

Some readers—academic historians in particular—could not agree, arguing that on the contrary, fiction was one genre with its own rules and biography or history dependent on fact another matter entirely. Keep that distinction clearly in mind, they admonished, and keep the two worlds separate. "Above all, don't forever be wandering the middle ground between them." A judgment rendered and advice given and duly rejected. Stegner would continue to warp, bend, and shape to his own purposes the world of direct experience in all three of his future novels. But first there was the biography of his friend Benny DeVoto to write.

Reprise

Overleaf: Noonday rest in Marble Canyon. (From *The Exploration of the Colorado River and Its Canyons*, J. W. Powell, 1895.)

I ⤸

In his prefatory note to *The Uneasy Chair: A Biography of Bernard DeVoto*, published in 1974, Wallace Stegner told of the discovery that had shaped his account of his friend's life and career. This was the growing realization as he read DeVoto's letters and manuscripts, which he had urged Stanford to house, that their life's work and outlook on the world had been remarkably similar. A sense of virtual identification with his friend's views and values he had experienced at certain moments all his life. "But until I began this biography I had not realized how many of my basic attitudes about the West, about America in general, about literature, and about history parallel his, either because so much of our experience retraced the same curve, or because of his direct influence."

Yet when Avis DeVoto approached him after her husband's death with the suggestion that he undertake the biography, Stegner had been reluctant for several reasons. In the first place, his mercurial friend would defy attempts to contain him inside the covers of a book. No one knew better than Stegner how contentious, difficult, and downright cruel but also supportive, friendly, and even loving DeVoto had been throughout a lifetime of constant quarreling. The ill-fitting parts of the man seemed impossible to assemble in a single portrait. How to deal with the legion of enemies DeVoto had made? Or the neuroses and phobias that had plunged him into recurrent moods of depression? Or his insistence on holding personal grudges? Then there was the problem of their close friendship itself. Stegner's son Page traced the difficulty his father encountered in recreating the life of his friend to the nearly exact parallels in their careers so that "when he created DeVoto's life, he created his own."

In 1968, however, thirteen years after Benny's death Stegner changed his mind as he contemplated retirement from teaching and the prospects of freelancing with its accompanying uncertainties. He wrote Avis DeVoto asking whether she was still interested in having him write the biography. With her assurance and willingness to lend a hand in the initial stages of collecting and recollecting he set to work, finishing his magisterial account five years later.

André Maurois once observed that "biography is a means of expression when the author has chosen his subject in order to respond to a secret need in his own nature." Stegner was content to attribute his choice to the influence of particular people or places, an impulse more personal than scholarly. "I wouldn't have written Powell if I hadn't known the Southern Utah plateaus," he explained later to Richard Etulain, "and I wouldn't have written Benny DeVoto's biography unless I had known him. All the history and biography I've done has been an offshoot of personal experiences and personal acquaintances." As the study of his friend's life began to take shape in his mind, however, he realized that something more pressing was involved—a deeper urge to explain DeVoto, not as a model of reformist behavior but as a teacher and an exemplar of total commitment to a cause in which he himself also believed. And just as DeVoto had fought angrily against the corporations liquidating his West during the Eisenhower years so now it fell to him to check the counterrevolutionary attack on the environment already building toward the Reagan administration's full-scale war on nature. Like his mentor, Stegner would meet the reactionary Republican challenge first with irritation and then with mounting anger that fed a new belligerence. Perhaps, as he still believed, the West represented a "geography of hope," but with each passing year in the late seventies and eighties that hope seemed to grow more forlorn as he himself traced the downward course of his late friend's career.

There were other difficulties in writing DeVoto's biography, as Stegner soon realized. "For one thing," he explained to an interviewer, "it presents you with the problem of how much to tell: things that are nobody's damn business," details that could embarrass DeVoto's widow or his friends and that had no necessary connection with his subject's actual work. "In my case," he continued, "it was Benny's career, the way his head worked and what he did with his head." Admittedly DeVoto had been terribly insecure and had managed to alienate a great many people, but that wasn't the point. "I wanted to write about the great things this flawed man produced out of his personal turmoil." Those "great things" were just the achievements Stegner himself had always aspired to: a strong grasp of the complications involved in writing history, a commanding knowledge of the West, and a genius for romantic narrative.

Despite his decision not to psychoanalyze his friend, Stegner was driven to seek a clue that satisfactorily explained DeVoto's contrary nature, and this he found in his subject's life in exile. DeVoto's career as a permanent outsider had begun in Ogden with a boyhood spent on the fringes of respectability and social acceptance, a hunger for which he carried east with him into a competitive intellectual world where he continued to struggle for both while publicly disdaining them. Just here, Stegner realized, author and subject had parted company. His own personal history was a case of the exile's return to home ground after exploring the Eastern cultural terrain, settling in a home in Los Altos and a summer homestead in the Vermont hills. In DeVoto he recognized an alternative self whose career led him away from his native region but whose understanding of its contradictions matched his own. In heading west after his New England excursion Stegner had enjoyed the good fortune of teaching writing on his own terms in a prestigious university. Denied the same chance at Harvard yet unwilling to return to the region he continued to write about, DeVoto had substituted research—in documents, diaries, memoirs, letters, and histories—in maintaining firsthand familiarity with the West. Stegner used his California home in the Los Altos hills as a base of operations for exploring Western mountains, rivers, and high country, which he described with unmatched visual power. DeVoto's investigatory base had been his Cambridge study where, with only an occasional foray west, he examined the documents and pored over the maps he needed to trace routes, locate places, measure distances, and stage events.

Nevertheless, both men had drawn on their Utah backgrounds in fashioning their conservationist creed, the primary article of which was the knowledge that west of the 100th meridian aridity called the tune. Both had read the Texas historian Walter Prescott Webb and had him to thank for their measured view of drylands possibilities. Webb, whose *The Great Plains* and subsequent *Divided We Stand: The Crisis of Frontierless Democracy* appeared during the Great Depression, defined the arid West as a "semi-desert with a desert heart," a description with which De Voto and Stegner agreed. Dryness, Webb explained, was the "dominating force" spreading like a "gigantic fire" out to the "desert-rim" country of West Texas, eastern Washington, and western North Dakota. Webb confirmed for DeVoto and Stegner their estimate of their home region as a "land of deficiencies . . . full of negatives and short on positives." For those settlers and small ranchers who tried to eke out a living in the Arid Region, scarce rainfall dictated the terms on which they succeeded or failed. It was these hardy souls working unpromising land that engaged first Webb and then DeVoto and Stegner. All three were primarily concerned with the region's little people.

With the end of the war in 1945 DeVoto's and Stegner's definition of the little people of America had broadened to include hundreds of thousands of new tourists and travelers freed once again to hit the road for a view of their country. Early in their careers both men, like the original advocates of Populism, had rested their analysis on a view of the West as—in DeVoto's words—a "plundered province," financially and culturally exploited, a colonial dependency captive to giant Eastern corporations and banks. Stegner confessed to having arrived at maturity "like most of my fellows to some extent a regional patriot. People in unfashionable or provincial places are made to feel a sort of colonial complex," he later admitted in explaining his and his subject's similar regional defensiveness.

The original Populist creed had been recycled during the Great Depression and given dramatic point by the forced departure of defeated High Plains farmers to the West Coast. As Stegner recalled in his biography, DeVoto's 1930s articles "brilliantly illuminate the ways in which a place and a society, even a half-formed one, can influence and mould individuals." Guided by the signposts that Walter Prescott Webb had planted throughout Depression dustbowls, DeVoto had described the West for readers of *Harper's* as a prisoner of Eastern business. "Throughout the West," he complained in 1934, "absentee ownership has channeled wealth out of the communities that produced it. . . . Throughout the West land

and power and minerals have been cash crops, and unspeakable stupidity, waste, corruption, and cynicism have sometimes gone into the harvesting of them." A modified version of this early indictment could be found thirty-five years later in Stegner's introduction to *The Sound of Mountain Water* (1969), where he described Western experience as "a history of resources often mismanaged and of compelling conditions often misunderstood or disregarded. . . . Here the trials were sometimes terrible for those who suffered them, and the errors did permanent damage to the land."

With the end of World War II and the return of prosperity, the old Populist complaints about colonialism and feudal dependency came to seem less relevant in an age of revived nationalism and prosperity. The war had turned DeVoto's and Stegner's dryland democracy into a homegrown corporate fiefdom. The people of this new West now appeared to suffer from an acute case of schizophrenia—"forever in rebellion," according to DeVoto after his trip west in 1946, yet all too willing to cooperate with the exploiters against themselves. For both DeVoto and Stegner the single remnant of the original Populism in the new age of corporate consolidation had been the dimming vision of an alternative community—a country in the mind held together by cooperative values, social responsibility, participatory ceremonies, and collective purpose which it called on the federal government to foster and protect. That shared vision, Stegner now understood as he struggled to finish the biography of his friend, had also been the strongest cord in their lifelong friendship.

Midway in his account of his friend's life Stegner paused to describe at length the turning point in DeVoto's outlook that followed his tour of the West in 1946. DeVoto, nervous and apprehensive as usual, had prepared for his trip by contacting the director of the National Park Service and the chief forester of the Forest Service for directions and advice. He also wrote to various friends throughout the region who could be counted on to ease the strain of constant travel and unanticipated inconveniences. "Jittery as the greenest tourist," according to Stegner, DeVoto was nevertheless convinced at the end of his adventure that the trip had been "the best thing I ever did in my life."

Stegner understood that until 1946 Benny's knowledge of the wider West was largely secondhand, derived from books and maps rather than personal experience. "He knew the narrow Wasatch front," Stegner recalled, "but little else: even of the country he had visited, he had up to 1946 only the briefest acquaintance, and there were whole regions he did not know at all." The '46 trip changed all that. DeVoto and Avis vastly enjoyed playing tourists, sharing the driving, stopping frequently to take in the magnificent scenery and consult with its protectors in the Forest and Park Services. He paid particular attention to highway conditions and roadside amenities in the new motel civilization spreading throughout the postwar West. He stored up advice for automakers on air conditioning, shock absorbers, and sun visors to make driving a more pleasurable experience. As a self-appointed consumer critic he had intended to speak knowledgeably to the new American tourist eager to discover America.

Tourism gave DeVoto renewed access to the West he had abandoned, its parks, reserves, and wilderness—"the desert in particular," Stegner remembered, "that green sagebrush waste rising in long alluvial skirts to the worn ranges." His initiation into tourism reinforced his conviction that the public domain—a national commons—belonged to all Americans who now were free to enjoy but also obligated to protect their inheritance. At last after five years of scenic deprivation they could take to the road again and reclaim their land. Yet all along his zigzag route Park and Forest personnel told him of threatened raids on public lands by organized grazing interests intent on "taking back" what they never owned. The combination of a tourist's sense of entitlement to the public domain and DeVoto's sudden realization that his own rights were being rudely challenged, Stegner could see from the distance of a quarter of a century, had handed him his last and greatest cause. The trip turned his friend into a crusader, "one of the most effective in our history." He had gone west as a tourist and returned an "embattled conservationist."

As he told the story of that early trip Stegner remembered that same year, 1946, when he too had taken to the road, "doing what a good third of America" was doing but on his own spartan terms. Together with Mary, young Page, a microbiologist "backroad fiend" and his wife, he had headed east through the Sierras into the "bald-assed desert" country on an extended camping trip. Stegner's was a different kind of tourist hunger—in 1946 and later. He always had the urge to get off the highway and up into the high country to renew acquaintance with his own past in "a hundred things once known and long forgotten." While DeVoto had been enjoying the amenities of travel, staying in motels, sampling small-town bars and restaurants, and making only occasional visits to the national parks and forests preserves, Stegner and his party of adventurers had camped in the sand in sagebrush country, traveling light with sleeping bags, water, and campfire food.

Early on, Stegner sensed more clearly than his friend the real significance of tourism and had estimated more accurately its potential for both good and evil. From now on, he reported to readers of the *Saturday Review of Literature* on his return, the typical tourist was likely to be a carbon copy of a middle-aged denizen of a trailer park who pulled in with his oversized camper, hooked up a variety of electrical gadgets, and unfolded his collapsible white picket fence to mark the bounds of his temporary residence—a 10-by-20 piece of Peoria, Illinois.

Nor had Stegner approved of the "curiously hectic metabolic rate" of postwar Nevada towns careening back and forth between hibernation and hysteria. Las Vegas, already in 1946 intent on becoming the gaming capital of the world, was all "glitter, glass, and chrome," every other building a casino "with a one-armed bandit reaching out to shake hands." Throughout the entire Arid Region developers, like spiders, were weaving their webs along the edges of the desert, building Bide-a-wees and Shangri-Las to house the growing hordes of tourists. The shores of mountain lakes were lined with ugly cottages squatting at the water's edge. Now, as Stegner began work on his biography of DeVoto twenty-five years later, it was clear to him that his own more intimate knowledge of the West had given him a sharper sense of the destructive powers of tourism and development than his friend had felt. Tourism was openly democratic, to be sure, and, properly managed, could continue to teach Americans to care for their land. But the underside of tourism was the developmental damage it had been doing to wilderness ever since 1946. By 1971 the dual nature of tourism was entirely clear: the American tourist was at one and the same time a would-be protector and a proven destroyer of the environment.

The heaviest costs levied by tourism were the roads that brought eager sightseers to and from the wilderness, and Stegner's case against them, of long standing, grew angrier as his fears for his intermountain country became more intense. It was his beloved desert that he sought to save from developers and improvers intent on servicing the tourists at a profit. Gradually as he approached the grim Reagan years he came to distinguish between parks and wilderness, between a national commons open to anyone and pristine country not readily approachable. Both were essential to the health of the citizenry but in different ways. Parks—generally forested and improved with paths and carriage roads, trails and markers—were a natural source of recreation and renewal for millions of Americans in need of refreshment. Wilderness, on the other hand, filled a deeper spiritual need that transcended the merely restorative. Wilderness meant silence, isolation, diminution of self—landscape both lovely and terrible—"such a wilderness Christ and the prophets went out into . . . harshly and beautifully colored," eroded by the elements through eons. "Save a piece of country like that intact," he insisted, "and it does not matter in the slightest that only a few people every year will go into it. That is precisely its value. Roads would be a desecration, crowds would ruin it." Those people unable or unequipped to enter the wilderness can survey its expanse from distant vantage points. "And if they can't even get to places on the Aquarius Plateau where the present roads will carry them, they can simply contemplate the *idea*, take pleasure in the fact that such a timeless and uncontrolled part of the earth is still there." Theirs would be a country in the mind, visualized yet real.

The most immediate threat to Stegner's wilderness silence came from the road builders equipped with federal and state money and taking their orders from developers and promoters as they smashed their way into the wilderness with logging and mining roads and scenic overlooks. After her husband's death Mary discovered an unpublished manuscript of Wally's written in 1966 that he must have considered too strong for publication. He had written the diatribe to protest the construction of a road along Glen Canyon proposed by the Utah Highway Commission. Why build this monstrosity? he had demanded and then provided an answer weighted with heavy sarcasm. "So people coming up dammed Glen Canyon can get out of the water and make it more easily from ramp to ramp. And anyone on the fringes of that lovely stone wilderness will hear their motors ten, fifteen, twenty miles away." Once there had been nothing to break the silences; soon there would be nothing to muffle the noise. "This road as proposed," he had written, taking his cue from his old friend Benny DeVoto, "would be a tragedy, the dimmest of 'wilderness breaking.'" A poverty program and public works for the region? "Yes, poverty of intelligence, poverty of imagination, poverty of vision, poverty of sensibility."

II 〰

By the time *The Uneasy Chair* appeared in 1974 it was clear that tourists formed the avant-garde of a huge invading force pouring into the Arid Region. DeVoto's and Stegner's home country was undergoing a massive inmigration, part of a national demographic shift. The dramatic change resulting from this intrusion would occupy Stegner for the rest of his life. Statistics underscore the significance of the shift. The number of people living along the Colorado Plateau, for example, doubled between 1960 and 1990 and increased 15 percent between 1990 and 1994. Annual growth rates since 1960 averaged 3.9 for Nevada, 3.1 for Idaho, 2.9 for Colorado, 2.7 for Utah and Arizona, and 2.2 for New Mexico—increases which have continued to rise since Stegner's death in 1993. In other words, the intermountain West has grown at a rate that exceeds that of Mexico and rivals that of sub-Saharan Africa.

Many of the new arrivals brought with them an alien lifestyle and a determination to pursue it in a region resistant to their notions of opulence and control. Up and down the intermountain West there suddenly appeared "pseudo-rural landscapes," as they were called, filled with "ranchettes" carved out of the cattle ranches of owners eager to sell their land and their way of life for a profit. In the two decades after 1978 Colorado farmland declined by ninety thousand acres a year. Farmland platted for subdivision between 1969 and 1987 in Park County, Wyoming, reached 19 percent; in Teton County, Idaho, 16 percent; in Gallatin County, Montana, 23 percent. As Stegner and his environmentalist friends throughout the Mountain West looked on in disbelief and dismay an altered landscape emerged out of these sales and transfers, whole sections consisting of evenly spaced 20-by-40 parcels, which Richard Knight, one of Stegner's good friends, described as lying across the countryside "like a gigantic grid, as if a giant prison door had fallen flat upon the earth."

Many of the plots of unpromising ground were graced with the "trophy homes" of the new and restless rich, huge excrescences rising from treeless bluffs and silhouetted against empty sky. Stegner led the chorus of critics of such pretentiousness with a blistering commentary. In an opening anecdote in "Striking the Rock," perhaps the best-known of his environmental essays collected in *The American West as Living Space* (1987), he skewered the pretensions to grandeur of the new rich and their obedient architects. The indictment begins with an interview of the proud designer of one of the new desert mansions who has just proved to his satisfaction that with enough money and technical expertise he could impose his grandiose vision "on any site, in any clime." To prove his point he had dropped his creation on a "waterless pale desert, spotted with shad scale and creosote bushes and backed by barren lion-colored mountains." Here sat a pile of dazzling white Bauhaus cubes hard by an immense lake-size swimming pool in the middle of acres of bright green lawn dotted with royal palms imported from Santa Barbara. Stegner had refrained from telling the architect that he thought his desert monstrosity immoral, that it "exceeded limits" and offended his sense "not of the possible but the desirable." "The only reasons for building there were to let mad dogs and rich men go out in the midday sun, and let them own and dominate a view they admired." In its challenge to the countryside the house struck him as both caricature and commentary on what Americans had been doing for over a century. "Instead of adapting, as we began to do, we have tried to make the countryside and the climate over to fit our existing habits and desires. Instead of listening to the silence, we have shouted into the void."

If the sins of the rich were on public display in their dysfunctional mansions, so were those of the lesser breed of new settlers, those entrepreneurs and developers crowding the fringes of the national parks, hemming them in with condominiums and tract housing, malls and onestops. In the suburban and exurban settings like Stegner's Los Altos home the losses were palpable and intensely personal. "We are living with remnants," he reported gloomily in the 1980s. Feral housecats had killed all the gophers and field mice, and the last pair of great horned owls died in his yard, victims of poisoned carrots put out by the neighbors.

Searching for the meaning of such drastic change, Stegner pondered the future in the form of pointed questions. Would the family ranch of the little man be absorbed by banks and financial institutions looking for tax write-offs? What would happen to the big corporate ranches? Would ranchers sell off their cattle and seek more profitable uses for their land—in "dudes, summer cottages, subdivisions, vacation condominiums?" Was it possible to stop entrepreneurs from continuing to build Big Skys, Ski Yellowstones, and more Sun Valleys? He admitted to asking questions he already knew the answers to.

Yet with his long-standing inclination to find the middle ground between premonitions of disaster and hopeless naïveté, Stegner professed to see both good news as well as bad in the rural migration. The influx seemed a mixed blessing—"for the newcomer hunting tranquility and self-determination as for the townsman whose community is invaded." Those new arrivals bent on exploitation brought bad news for everyone, themselves most of all. But even the more responsible newcomers, though they changed their location, seldom altered their ethics or ambitions, their politics or their social habits. In their flight from overcrowded suburbias all migrants tend to reproduce the very problems they seek to escape. Taxes go up, the price of housing soars, the costs of policing, sewerage, and schooling mount. "Oldtimers can't afford to keep their own places. Somebody gets the idea of attracting tourists. Craftspeople follow the tourists, and more tourists follow the craftspeople." The downward spiral ends in the loss of integrity and then the identity of the original community. That, at least, was Stegner's worst-case scenario. Was there another?

Stegner himself recognized the pessimistic drift of his thinking, his emphasis now on the defenses needed against commercialism, sprawl, gentrification, on the one hand, and ongoing exploitation of the region's resources by oil companies, lumber giants, mining syndicates, on the other. Against the host of intruders he recommended a planning strategy contrived to assure at least a measure of harmony with their natural surroundings for oldtimers and newcomers alike. "But these ways require that we exhibit forethought and planning and aesthetic sensitivity, and they also require, particularly in this day and age, that we abandon the notion that a

property owner can do anything he pleases with his property simply because he owns it and because that's the way it has always
been." The biggest bugaboo of all remained the old "don't tread on
me" Western outlook on the world. To counter that throwback to
nineteenth-century myths Americans would need a new consciousness of the need for ecosystem management monitored by
the federal government and its various agencies.

What were the odds that effective agency management of the
ecosystem could ever become a reality? Stegner's hopes were originally fairly high for a renaissance in rural America and a small-town
revival with its promise of renewed family life, occupational
integrity, and social responsibility—values now threatened unless
its inhabitants woke up and defended themselves. By 1980—
before the election of Ronald Reagan—it seemed to him that in
the decade since Earth Day, signs had appeared pointing to a
change in American expectations for protecting the environment—"an alteration of the free land and unregulated
individualism myths still clung to so desperately by the sagebrush
rebels and 'New Federalists.'" In the preceding fifteen years or
so, environmentalists had been joined by millions of Americans
who had learned a new respect for the land and acquired a new
consciousness of their relationship to it. "At long last it seems
that ordinary citizens have become less commonly raiders and
more commonly conservers and stewards of the only continent
they are ever going to possess." Part of this new consciousness, he
reasoned, was the work of the environmental groups themselves,
their publications, growing memberships, effective lobbying, and
increased pressure on the federal agencies charged with managing the ecosystem. Admittedly these federal bureaus and
agencies left much to be desired as enforcers and planners. Turf
wars were all too common, and priorities shifted radically with

changes in political party government. "Nevertheless, this is the best protection we have, and it is not to be disparaged." All Americans, but Westerners in particular, needed to ask themselves some questions. Half of the West remains in the hands of these same federal agencies. What, then, should they do?

Do they exist to provide bargain-basement grass to favored stockmen whose grazing privileges have become all but hereditary, assumed and bought and sold along with the title to the home spread? Are they the hired exterminators of wildlife? Is it their function to negotiate loss-leader coal leases with energy conglomerates, and to sell timber below cost to Louisiana Pacific? Or should they be serving a much larger public purpose whose outdoor recreation of backpacking, camping, fishing, hunting, river-running, mountain climbing, hang-gliding, and God help us, dirt biking, are incompatible with clear-cut forests and overgrazed poison-baited, and strip-mined grasslands? Or is there a still higher duty—to maintain the health and beauty of the lands they manage, protecting from everybody . . . the watershed and spawning streams, forests and grasslands, geological and scenic splendors, historical and archeological and scenic remains, air and water and serene space, that once led me, in a reckless moment, to call the western public lands part of the geography of hope?

Answers to these policy questions lay squarely in the realm of Western history, which Stegner, together with DeVoto, had been exploring all his life and to which in the closing years of his career he returned with a seemingly unending spate of environmental articles, essays, lectures, collections, and collaborations. The ten years before his death in 1993 saw an unprecedented number of such appeals, all of them informed by a deepening awareness of historical determinants. All his life he had argued the case for the indispensability of the historical consciousness as a bridge or lifeline connecting knowledge of the past to an understanding of present conditions and plans for the future. Now with a sense of urgency sharpened by the unforgivable mismanagements of the Reagan administration, he sought to drive home to readers the real meaning and relevance of that past. Building on the research he had gathered for his study of John Wesley Powell and a mounting pile of recent environmental histories, he began his own reconstruction of conservation thought and activity since the days of George Perkins Marsh and Henry David Thoreau in the middle years of the nineteenth century. His accounts frequently opened with an apology for his belated education in environmentalism. "I guess I was pretty innocent," he admitted, " . . . because I hadn't ever put my mind to problems." World War II had prevented him from getting out into the country and seeing for himself, and at Harvard and Wisconsin where he had taught, the problems of land use and environmental management had gone virtually unacknowledged. Like most Americans including his friend DeVoto, he had cheered the construction of Hoover Dam and welcomed the growing number of irrigation projects. "I guess I just accepted the habits of mind of most people in Utah at the time that this was progress—lots of jobs."

It had taken the end of the war and the sudden arrival on the Western scene of the disillusioned gunslinger Bernard DeVoto to convince him otherwise and show him the need to reconstruct his own American past. In "A Capsule History of Conservation," compiled from his reading of early and contemporary environmentalists and published in the *Smithsonian* magazine in 1990, he surveyed the historical terrain, documenting the "slow revolution in values" which had made the present environmental movement possible. Humans had required only two hundred years, according to his calculations, to turn the Puritan wilderness filled with howling savages and wild beasts into the late twentieth century's wilderness islands besieged on all sides by advancing civilization. The pathway to modernity had been strewn with a series of myths and stereotypes of hardy frontiersman and untrammeled individualism—from James Fenimore Cooper's "Leatherstocking" onward. "Wilderness man cannot live with settlement man," or so it had seemed to Stegner as he surveyed the advance of the frontier in the nineteenth century. Emerson's view of a divine Nature teaching mankind had conflicted with his celebration of self-reliance and unfettered individual energy. Environmentalism really began with two other Yankees: George Perkins Marsh and Henry David Thoreau. Marsh, a son of Vermont, had witnessed the destruction of the state's forests and the ensuing erosion along its river banks, and in his classic *Man and Nature* (1864) had traced the consequences of deforestation on an enlarged scale in the Mediterranean basin. Stegner had a clearer understanding of Marsh's contribution to ecology than he did of Thoreau's experience of the wilderness. He was fully convinced by Marsh's description of man as the "disturbing agent" and destroyer of natural harmonies. Stegner also appreciated Thoreau's defense of wildness but lacked familiarity with his accounts of several trips into the Maine woods and his lonely ascent of Mount Katahdin where he encountered wilderness as the looming presence of Chaos and Old Night.

In recounting the early history of American environmental thought Stegner noted that the "tracing of ideas is a guessing game" and that radical ideas have been around for centuries unrecognized, their warnings unheeded. "Only if they win a substantial approval and give visible effects do they achieve a plan or even a predictable curve of development." He proceeded to trace this upward path through the contributions of his heroes from Marsh and Thoreau to Powell and Muir and on to twentieth-century pioneers Benton MacKaye, Bob Marshall, Rachel Carson, Howard Zahniser, and the greatest of them all, Aldo Leopold with his land ethic and Bernard DeVoto with his determination to practice it. Here were the leaders who had pointed the way on the "long road the nation has traveled to get to Earth Day and beyond."

Just what impact on the public mind had these environmental spokesmen and activists made? What results in the formulation of policies and approaches? Stegner offered the establishment of Yellowstone National Park as an early example: a group of outdoorsmen with money and political connections had camped out in its precincts and promptly agreed to help set it aside. They took their case to Washington, D.C., where Congress responded to their lobbying by voting to establish the first national park. Similarly, congressional authorization of forest reserves resulted from the complaints of early preservationists and the horrific example of the clear-cutting of northern Michigan forests. Once empowered, Presidents Harrison and Cleveland and then, more dramatically, Theodore Roosevelt took advantage of the grant of congressional power and set aside a growing number of forest reserves. When a Republican-dominated Congress had second thoughts in 1907 and forbade further presidential proclamations, Teddy Roosevelt and his chief forester, Gifford Pinchot, sat up late one night and, poring over maps and surveys, first signed into law twenty-one new national forests, and only then signed the bill that would have prevented him. Roosevelt also established the first wildlife refuge in 1903, thus fulfilling the life's work of outdoorsman and editor George Bird Grinnell. John Muir's contributions to conservation are the stuff of legend, but not so Benton MacKaye's dream of an Appalachian Trail and his untiring efforts, together with Bob Marshall and the Wilderness Society, to put it through. Looming large in Stegner's pantheon of environmental heroes was Aldo Leopold whose concept of a land ethic provided environmentalists with a clearer understanding of the scientific basis for their ecological thinking and the need to preach individual responsibility.

Aldo Leopold's was the spirit presiding over the union of environmentalism and ecology in the second half of the twentieth century. Born and bred on the Iowa side of the Mississippi in Burlington, Leopold received a degree in forestry from Yale in 1909 and promptly joined Gifford Pinchot's Forest Service as a forest assistant in District Three, which comprised what were then the territories of New Mexico and Arizona. As an avid sportsman, he soon became concerned with the need for game management, a concern that his superiors in the service did not share. At the same time, however, he subscribed to the widely held belief of hunters and stockmen everywhere in the importance of exterminating predators—wolves, mountain lions, and the like—in order to protect various species of grazing animals, a view he came to repudiate wholly as he gradually recognized all nature as an interlocking community. In 1924 he settled in Madison, Wisconsin, where he served in the service's Forest Products Laboratory and then joined the faculty of the university as a specialist in game management. Here he acquired an ecological conscience based on the premise of land as an organism—an intricate web containing all life. Out of this conviction came his "land ethic," which required all individuals to treat their environments "in terms of what is ethically and esthetically right, as well as what is economically expedient." Leopold's land ethic simply enlarged the boundaries of the good community to include water, soils, plants, and animals or as he put it, "collectively the land." "A land ethic, then, reflects the existence of an ecological conscience, and this in turn reflects a conviction of individual responsibility for the health of the land." Here was the challenge that Leopold left to the conservation movement at his untimely death in 1948, just as Bernard DeVoto took up the task of explaining its consequences for a postwar generation.

A further broadening of popular understanding of ecology and the dangers to the environment in the widespread use of pesticides arrived with the appearance in 1963 of Rachel Carson's *Silent Spring*, a hard-hitting indictment of the chemical industry that DeVoto would have fully appreciated. In all of these cases and others as well, Stegner was convinced, it was the work of individuals or small groups of the like-minded and ethically driven who had found the energy and mounted the pressure that, however partially and belatedly, was producing crucial environmental protection.

Just as Bernard DeVoto had distinguished two Republican parties—the conservation-minded faithful gathered around Theodore Roosevelt and Gifford Pinchot and the regional party spoilsmen bent on undoing their accomplishments—so thirty years later Stegner made a similar distinction between agencies of the federal government and their varied responses to public pressure for environmental protection. There were agencies like the National Forest Service, product of Pinchot's philosophy of "wise use," which quickly became captive of the very logging interests it was designed to control. Across the twentieth century the Forest Service had turned into a hostile and increasingly surly opponent of meaningful environmental regulation, a glaring example of the vulnerability of federal regulatory agencies to the whims of the politicians. Just as Eisenhower's appointment of Mormon patriarch Ezra Taft Benson as secretary of agriculture plunged Bernard DeVoto into deepening doubt as to the future of environmental protection, so thirty years later Reagan's choice of James Watt as secretary of the interior angered Stegner and appalled the environmental camp. Stegner complained bitterly that Watt was doing the dirty work of the Sagebrush Rebels who wanted to eliminate the Bureau of Land Management and seize all of the grazing lands overseen by the Forest Service. Reagan gave the Rebels James Watt, who installed as head of the Bureau of Land Management Robert Burford, who determined to pull all its regulatory teeth.

Back in the 1940s, when DeVoto and Stegner were being recruited to conservation, the activities of the Forest Service had appeared almost heroic in their eyes, and the service seemed to be the most responsible agency in Washington. But Eisenhower Republicanism gave the loggers a green light to clear-cut almost at will. Thus began nearly a half-century's adversarial relationship between the service and its environmental critics who continued to denounce it for its neglect and arrogance. "It really wants to cut wood more than anything else," Stegner observed in conversation with Richard Etulain in 1990, and little happened subsequently to alter his opinion. "Too many timber sales, too often at a loss of money as well as in other legitimate values, and far too much roading—roading being a preliminary to logging and a way of forestalling wilderness designation by spoiling the wilderness in advance."

All of the federal bureaus, Stegner realized, walked a narrow line between preservation and exploitation, hemmed in by the developmental pressures and regional opposition of powerful economic interests. The intermountain West, increasingly Republican since midcentury, continued to be the spiritual home of blue-sky developmentalism. And the cowardly lion among the federal bureaus, according to Stegner and the environmental community, was the Bureau of Reclamation which, he insisted, was really "something else." Once the object of DeVoto's and Stegner's admiration, the bureau had never lived up to its promise to serve the family farmer through scaled and well-managed irrigation projects. Instead it built mammoth dams with little or no thought given to their effects on watersheds. Underfunded for the first three decades of its existence, it received new life during the Depression and the Second World War. "It grew like a mushroom, like an exhalation," Stegner remembered. "By the 1940s the bureau, which only a few years before had been hanging on a shoestring, had built or was building the four greatest dams ever built on earth up to that time—Hoover, Shasta, Bonneville, and Grand Coulee—and was already the greatest force in the West."

The Bureau of Reclamation, which Stegner and David Brower had faced down in the controversy over the Echo Park dams, had quickly learned which side its bread was buttered on. "It had discovered where power was, and allied itself with it: with the growers and landowners, private and corporate, whose interests it served, and with the political delegations, often elected out of the same group, who carried the effort in Washington for more and more pork-barrel projects." On questions of water policy, political parties ceased to exist: "You cannot tell Barry Goldwater from Moe Udall, or Orrin Hatch from Richard Lamm."

At precisely this point of party collaboration the environmental opposition to federal government water policy appeared in full force. Scientific evidence on the killing of major rivers by ill-considered dam building had been piling up throughout the seventies— drowned canyons, ugly drawback reservoirs, side gulches choked with boulders and gravel, mud banks, surface salts, and alkali flats. By the eighties word was spreading that Western dams, far from the blessing they purported to be, were in fact monumentally destructive. In his heightened criticism Stegner drew on a growing literature on the environmental costs of the hydraulic society that Americans continued to build: Mark Reisner's popular *Cadillac Desert*; Donald Worster's massive *Rivers of Empire*. Their argument was distressingly simple—reckless irrigation of desert lands eventually increases desertification as nature takes back its own. A 1983 report of the Council on Environmental Quality warned that desertification in certain parts of the arid West was proceeding faster than in Africa.

Problems of land and water management continued to multiply throughout the 1980s as hostility to environmentalism mounted both within the Reagan administration and among its avid supporters in the intermountain West. Stegner found himself reassessing his initially sanguine outlook on federal government policy. The "depressing facts" he kept compiling added to his feelings of loss and longing for a time when the rivers ran free. "Sad to say, they make me admit, when I face them, that the West is no more the Eden I once thought it than the Garden of the World that the boosters and engineers tried to make it, and neither nostalgia nor boosterism can any longer make a case for it as the geography of hope."

Was hope, however diminished, anywhere to be found? Stegner provided part of the answer himself by stepping up his environmental activity on all levels—local, state, and national. He helped organize the Committee for Green Foothills in Los Altos in an attempt to save them from "county carelessness." The county seat was down in San José, and "nobody gave a damn about the foothills down there." Developers were running wild and tearing up the neighborhood. "We operated primarily to keep a sharp citizen's watch on planning commissions and town council meetings," he explained. He was also an active member of California Tomorrow, a statewide land-use planning group organized for the same defensive purposes. Also in the national Trust for Public Land and People for Open Space, as he continued to serve on the Advisory Board for National Parks, Historical Sites, Buildings, and Monuments while remaining fully engaged with Sierra Club and Wilderness Society business. Still, he continued to depreciate his worth to the movement by insisting that unlike Benny DeVoto he was not a particularly effective or eager agitator. He confessed to his friend T.H. Watkins that his meager contribution paled beside those of Dave Brower, Ed Wayburn, Howard Zahniser, and all "the hard-nosed, tough and durable types" throughout the movement. Activists and professionals like these were the real workers with "an immediate, practical, effective usefulness." "I never have," he insisted. "I am a paper tiger, Watkins, typewritten on both sides."

A paper tiger, perhaps, but hardly a toothless one. In the last fifteen years of his life Stegner wrote environmental articles and essays by the dozen, exceeding the output of Benny DeVoto in his last years. Some of the best he reprinted in four collections: *The Sound of Mountain Water* (1969, reissued in 1985); *One Way to Spell Man* (1982); *The American West as Living Space* (1987); and *Where the Bluebird Sings to the Lemonade Springs* (1992). His frustration and growing anger could be read in the title of these and other occasional pieces like the one for the Washington *Post* following the presidential election of 1980 which asked the rhetorical question "Will Reagan Ride with the Raiders?" and another that declared "If the Sagebrush Rebels Win, Everybody Loses" (*Living Wilderness*, Summer 1981). Disillusionment and disapproval could also be read in the titles of other popular articles—"Water Warnings, Water Futures," "Ask the Dust," and "The Spoiling of the American West." Increasingly it seemed to him that only vigorous lobbying for the wilderness could save Americans from the "termite life" they had made for themselves with factories, power plants, and resorts for the rich.

Nor did Stegner make any effort to hide his dissatisfaction with politicians and the public at large. "The number of functional illiterates that our free public education produces," he complained in a review of Aldo Leopold's land ethic, "does not make us sanguine about educating the majority of the public to respect the earth, a harder form of literacy." To his friends he confessed to feeling more than a bit bruised by his constant battling against the spoilers. "I think those sixteen years [between 1969 and 1985] have taken some skin off." Misled by the false promise of unlimited growth, Americans kept on building and wasting as though there were no tomorrow. "But you watch what's happened to what you're building, and I think you get a little jaundiced. What's happening, of course, is that big—enormous—and quite irresistible *money* has taken over the West. And resources—extractable resources—are what money is after." Moreover, Reagan's entire bureaucracy appeared to agree with James Watt that the country was simply a gigantic warehouse and that corporations and conglomerates were the Hanson Loaders and Dempster Dumpsters especially designed to empty it. What were environmentalists to do? His answer—save the remnants somehow. But the real question was how?

As exurbia crept up the slopes of Los Altos and developers swarmed across the Mountain West, the Stegners found summer solace in their upcountry enclave in Greensboro, Vermont, which they had first discovered in 1938 and which had grown in appeal ever since. "Salt Lake City next Tuesday for a speech," he reported in one of his frequent letters to former Stegner Fellow Ivan Doig, "and then we can escape to Vermont, which from here looks like a cool green sanctuary. Ah wilderness! There is too much frenzy and noise around here." In his early novella *Second Growth* (1947), Stegner's adventurous local boy leaves his crossroads village modeled on Greensboro eager for a look at the larger world yet saddened as "the trees closed softly around the backwards tracks like snow over footprints. . . . The world went on, incomprehensibly huge, and there were a thousand frontiers to be crossed." Forty years later that same upcountry Vermont, seemingly still lost to progress, cognizant of limits, and set in its ways, had only gained in meaning for the Stegners. In 1939, the Stegners bought a ramshackle farmhouse and barn on two hundred acres of pasture and woods, and Wallace began fixing up the place in between stints of writing. Page Stegner recalled helping his father plant hundreds of Norway pines, part of Wallace's ongoing restoration project. "For summers," Wallace Stegner told Richard Etulain, "I'd as soon be in Vermont or New Hampshire as anywhere in the world."

Vermont, which Stegner like DeVoto before him described as a large village democracy, served him as a prime example of the surviving remnant equipped with powers of endurance and regeneration. Unlike his arid West it could heal itself: you could "tear hell" out of its woods and they would recover. Stegner described this surviving landscape with unmatched clarity and precision. In his last novel, *Crossing to Safety*, set in Greensboro, he took readers up worn country roads rising into pines and firs. "Dust has whitened the ferns along the roadside, gypsy moths have built their tents in the chokeberry bushes, the meadow on the left is yellow with goldenrod, ice-blue with asters, stalky with mullein, rough with young spruce. Everything taller than the grass is snagged with white fluff of milkweed. On the other side is a level hayfield, green from a second cutting. The woods at the far edge rise in a solid wall." On the downhill return "the hill drops away, furred with raspberry and dense hardwood seedlings, to the

Ansel Adams, *Winter Sunrise, the Sierra Nevada, from Lone Pine, California* (1944). Wallace Stegner, who greatly admired Adams's art, explained his friend's genius as the uncanny ability to discern equivalence to nature where there are shapes but no forms. "Imagination transmutes shapes into forms, and technique painstakingly realizes the forms in the symbolic system of photographic art." (© ANSEL ADAMS PUBLISHING RIGHTS TRUST/CORBIS.)

untouched woods below. The view swoops down and then levels to the lake and its far meadows, then up again to broken hills, the blue mountain ridge, the sky with traveling snow-white clouds."

Stegner's mastery of color in his late novels gave him an understanding and a keen appreciation of the photography of his friend Ansel Adams, who constructed his massive forms in black and white. Stegner and Adams had become fast friends soon after they met in Santa Fe in 1946. Over the years they discovered that they had much in common—a love of the land, a distaste for confrontational politics, and a preference for quiet and unadorned discussions of art. In the 1980s both were vocal critics of the Reagan administration's James Watt, whom Stegner accused of giving away the store and whom Adams denounced as

"a dangerous influence in our society," reserving for the president himself the charge of being even more dangerously ignorant.

Beneath their forthrightness and geniality lay a shared aesthetic resting on a sense of form that Stegner recognized as the key to his friend's artistic genius. Stegner wrote four explanatory essays on Adams's photography in an attempt to teach viewers to see his work in the right light. Adams's photographs, he argued, were the creation not simply of a love of nature but of a strong sense of artistic limits—"the absolute reverse of effusive." Critics who persisted in placing Adams in the expansive tradition of Thomas Moran and Albert Bierstadt had it all wrong. "He sees with such austerity, even severity, that some have mistakenly called him cold." Adams approached his art with a keen awareness of the need for technical control that would come only with a mastery of *craft* and *language*—visual in Ansel's case, verbal in Wallace's own. Adams avoided romantic excess, Stegner argued, through a conviction that "limitation breeds expertise." Viewers of his work needed, first of all, to distinguish between Ansel Adams the environmentalist and Ansel Adams the artist. His environmental opinions were one thing, his artistic rendering of nature something entirely different. What Adams sees he sees *into* and discovers and then draws out of nature a "symbolic representation," which he renders, not with color but with "tones of brightness" from pure white to nearly pure black. With his own verbal mastery of color Stegner could see exactly what Adams's disciplined art achieved. "In nature, Adams points out, there are colors, brilliant or subtle, that every photographer must see as equivalents on the brightness scale of grays; and in nature there are—properly speaking—no forms, only shapes. Imagination transmutes shapes into forms, and technique painstakingly realizes the forms into the symbolic system of photographic art, so that a sheet of paper printed in values of gray can actually strike the viewer with more force than would the natural objects from which it was made."

An adolescence spent in the arid plateau country of southern Utah had furnished Stegner with a palette running from sulphur yellows and rusty ochers to sage greens and light blue washes. In *Angle of Repose*, Susan Burling Ward with her fine-tuned visual sense steps out into her yard to scan the "tumbled hills as bright as a lion's hide" and, turning, "she saw those five parallel spurs, bare gold on top, darkly wooded in the gulches, receding in layers of blue haze." For Ansel Adams, on the other hand, there were gray granite walls, deep cliff shadows, dark forests, and white clouds. Yosemite, Stegner could see, had taught his friend that "even the deepest shadow has half-perceived forms, just as the purest snow will be pregnant with implicit shadows, and that all the world's wonder lies between nearly black and nearly white."

As he grew older Stegner continued to exploit his own personal responses to wilderness landscape as he watched a massive in-migration and economic boom transform large parts of it. A cancerous population growth and development in the postwar decades was bringing the long history of the West to its culminating point. It is a curious fact that neither DeVoto nor Stegner ever attempted a full account of the rise of the modern West but contented themselves with fragments and outlines in their histories, essays, and articles, which sketched but never completed the story of spoliation they both knew by heart. At his death DeVoto left an uncompleted manuscript developing the themes of Western geography, climate, resources, politics, and myths, many of which he had already treated in his "Easy Chair" pieces. In looking over DeVoto's draft as he prepared to write his biography Stegner surmised that with enough reworking, for which DeVoto was famous, the manuscript might possibly have made "a powerful book." "But it seems to me more likely that it would have been a kind of *omnium gatherum*, a collection of things already said, and better, when the heat was on him." Here was an explanation, as well, for Stegner's preference for frequent collections of his own shorter pieces, selected with care and prefaced by a general statement of intent. To one of these collections, *The Sound of Mountain Water*, he affixed an introduction entitled "Some Geography, Some History," which followed DeVoto in tracing the outlines of the emergence of the modern West. Like DeVoto's brief accounts, the sketch tells the tale of a century of destruction and deterioration of the Western wilderness. Once the pine woods of upper Michigan and Wisconsin had been clear-cut, the lumber companies moved to Washington and Oregon and set up their sawmills in pristine coastal forests. When the great Mesabi Range showed signs of exhaustion, Utah and Wyoming took its place while Colorado awaited the depletion of petroleum reserves in the East. To the despoilers, Manifest Destiny meant massive destruction of the wilderness West, which served them as a gigantic grab bag.

The raids on the West's wilderness resources had begun with the Mountain Men who cleaned out the beaver in twenty short years before they lost their market in 1840. They were followed by a second set of raiders, miners greedy for the variety of metals to be had throughout the intermountain region—gold on Colorado's Cripple Creek and Clear Creek and Montana's Gold Creek, and coal, iron, and copper nearly everywhere else. "Montana, Colorado, most of Idaho and Nevada, all drew their first inhabitants to the mineralized mountains, not to their agricultural lands." Soon, however, the raid on the grasslands began, led by corporate owners from the East and across the Atlantic in England and Scotland. DeVoto's original charge had been correct: "The men who set out to get rich from Western grasslands shared the psychology—and the ignorance of consequences—of the men who had cleaned out the beaver, the buffalo, and the precious metals." Stegner improved on his friend's indictment with a series of self-answering questions:

Who among the mountain men would have paused to consider, or would have cared, that beaver were a water resource, and that beaver engineering was of great importance in the maintenance of stream flow and the prevention of floods? Who among the miners worried about what happened to the watersheds when they logged their timbers or tore up stream beds with their dredges? Who among the cattlemen knew or cared that in a dry land grass, like minerals, might be non-renewable . . . that overgrazing both prevented reseeding and encouraged erosion?

For over a hundred and fifty years the wilderness West, Stegner agreed with his friend, had served Americans as a huge treasure chest to be pried open by anyone with sufficient strength and greed. The history of those years, accordingly, was one of violence and endless quarreling among the various looters over land that none of them owned: Mountain Men against Native Americans; lumbermen against settlers; cattlemen against nesters. These internecine battles supplied Americans with the mythic materials and tall-in-the-saddle tales they seemingly craved, fictions that came complete with unlikely cowboy heroes. "Let them be lawless in defense of the law, unconventional in the service of convention, and the peculiarity of their ethics, like the dubiousness of their exploitation of the natural resources, blurs and disappears in a blaze of picturesqueness." The gospel of absolute individual ownership and the prospect of quick profits lives on in a tightly organized corporate world and threatens to wipe out what is left of the wilderness.

Across the years Stegner offered several different definitions of wilderness, not all of them congruent and some of them contradictory. History taught him an anthropocentric approach to wilderness as inextricably connected to humans. "A place is nothing in itself," he had told the readers of *This is Dinosaur*. "It has no meaning, it can hardly be said to exist, except in terms of human perception, use, and response." Dinosaur, he reasoned, should be protected against dam builders who wanted to destroy it, but left open to backpackers and river runners who respected it. Wilderness, in this definition, is there for sensible use, a source of refreshment and reinvigoration. The only check on wilderness behavior is the river rat Pat Lynch's reminder to "do no harm."

Stegner provided a second definition of wilderness, however, which was more restrictive and abstract. This definition appeared most famously in his "Wilderness Letter," which celebrated the virtue of pristine, unscarred, and potentially inviolate wilderness. "The idea alone sustains me," he wrote. "Save a piece of country like that intact, and it does not matter in the slightest that only a few people every year will go into it. That is precisely its value." The rest of the American community can find inspiration in the mere fact of its undefiled existence. Wilderness, in short, as pure ideal.

Yet on occasion Stegner would veer off in the direction of Frederick Jackson Turner's democratic celebration of wilderness and frontier. This wilderness challenged and tested the pioneers who crossed or settled it, hardy men and women of his and DeVoto's telling who pulled up stakes in the East, headed into the unknown, and were baptized by adversity and ultimately strengthened by it. Stegner, like DeVoto before him, departed from Turner's celebration of democratic individualism by emphasizing the collective and communal results of frontier experience—the building of homes, neighborhoods, and towns. Still, the notion of wilderness as a trial of strength—"something that has helped form our character"—sat uneasily beside the promise of spiritual renewal—the "need to learn to listen to the land, hear what it says."

Stegner's most powerful evocations of wilderness came from his personal experiences, which he worked into both his fiction and his essays. In a memorable short story, "Two Rivers," there is a young boy's panoramic view from a canyon gateway emptying into endless prairie running out to the mountains of western Montana. "They were far above the world he knew. The air was cleaner, thinner. There was cold water running from the rocks, and all around were trees. And over the whole canyon, like a haze in the clear air, was that other thing, that memory or ghost of a memory." In Havasu Canyon, wilderness discloses itself in a welcome moment. "At every turn the tight-enclosed canyon stirs with a breath of freshness, and we look ahead hopefully, but each time the walls close in around a new turn. . . . Then suddenly, swift and quiet and almost stealthy, running a strange milky blue over pebbles like gray jade, Havasu Creek comes out of nowhere."

Ansel Adams helped Stegner see wilderness in its sweep and grandeur, but it was Aldo Leopold and Wendell Berry who provided the land ethic needed to protect not only wild but more settled country as well. Leopold's land ethic with its call for individual stewardship carried Stegner out of wilderness into parks and preserves filled with tourists and on into working lands interspersed with suburbia and exurbia, and ultimately to the city itself. The crucial linkage was provided by Leopold's ethical imperative, which applied to any and all environments whether in inner-city community gardens, suburban green space, nature paths, or riverbanks leading up watersheds into pristine rugged terrain called wilderness. A land ethic which mandated stewardship, Leopold announced, "changes the role of *Homo sapiens* from conqueror of the land-community to plain member and citizen of it." Stegner expanded Leopold's directive to embrace the whole of the American land. "We need an environmental ethic that will reach all the way from the preservation of untouched wilderness to the beautification of industrial cities, that will concern itself with saving the still-savable and healing the half-ruined and cleansing the polluted, that will touch not only land but air and water, that will have as its purpose the creation of a better environment for men, as well as the creation or preservation of viable habitats for the species that our expansion threatens."

Here was Stegner's answer to both environmental purists and relativists. From one side beginning in the 1980s came warnings from a younger generation of deep ecologists who cautioned their elders against anthropocentrism, the tendency to place human beings at the center of their thought and action. To them Stegner openly confessed his weakness, if that was what it amounted to: "But I know no other way to look at the world, settled or wild, except through my own human eyes." He knew full well that the world had not been specially created for his benefit, and he was willing to share the guilt for its misuse. "But I am the only instrument that I have access to by which I can enjoy the world and try to understand it."

A second charge came from another wing of environmental revisionists who complained that veterans like Stegner, in concentrating exclusively on wilderness preservation, were in danger of neglecting their own backyards. These neoconservationists, as they might be called, objected to what they considered misplaced emphasis. As William Cronon, one of their spokesmen and a sympathetic critic explains, "We mistake ourselves when we suppose that wilderness can be the solution to our culture's problematic relationships with the nonhuman world, for wilderness is itself no small part of the problem." Wilderness, according to Cronon and other commentators on traditionalism, is simply a cultural construct—a fiction or myth—inherited from the eighteenth century with its notion of the sublime. The idea of a sublime nature towering over mankind was particularly appealing to a rising class of townsmen—industrialists, bankers, and financiers—who were otherwise busy destroying what they presumably worshiped.

According to these historical-minded critics of wilderness worship the enticing mixture of awe and fear, wonder and terror, which wild landscape presumably inspired was precisely what a new industrial age was hell-bent on obliterating. In nineteenth-century American terms wilderness could signify the face of a benevolent God for John Muir and his citified followers or as an inscrutable Chaos and Old Night to Henry Thoreau standing alone on the summit of Mount Katahdin. In either case the sublime simply compensated for a projected loss of undisturbed nature. Whether viewing wilderness as cathedral or challenge, Victorian city dwellers credited it with a mystical power that comfortably diminished the stature of the self and lessened its materialist hunger. If such wilderness worship was not exactly phony, according to Cronon and the revisionists, it was nevertheless an attitude particularly congenial to an urban upper class. As Cronon puts it in his otherwise evenhanded assessment: "The dream of an unworked natural landscape is very much the fantasy of people who have never themselves had to work the land to make a living—urban folk for whom food comes from a super-market or a restaurant instead of a field, and for whom the wooden houses in which they live and work apparently have no meaningful connection to the forests in which trees grow and die." Abandoning this *ad hominem* argument in his conclusion, Cronon rests his case against the American tendency to "fetishize sublime places" on a plea for a better understanding of what is "natural." What Americans really need to do, he insists, is to

Wallace Stegner was an inveterate sojourner throughout the Arid Region who took every opportunity to study its austere landscape. He appears here in a photograph taken around 1960 enjoying the expansive view from a vantage point in Nevada's Black Rock Desert. (PHOTO: DAVID MILLER, COURTESY OF PAGE STEGNER.)

replace their belief in bipolarity with the idea of continuum—of nature as including cities and the middle ground right in our own midst.

If Stegner had been called upon to comment on such criticism, he might have done so—as he always had—by pointing to his own experience as an exception to the rule. Not all lovers of the wilderness were urban coupon cutters who periodically retired to the Adirondacks or Sun Valley. Admittedly there was an element of

Wallace Stegner loved and cared for all his land, both the upland country-side surrounding his summer place in Greensboro, Vermont, and the fields behind his home in Los Altos. This 1982 photograph was taken in the Los Altos Hills. (COURTESY OF PAGE STEGNER.)

truth in that blanket indictment, but he had spent a lifetime telling the larger story of environmental protection in which the rod-and-gun types played only a part. John Wesley Powell came from no such privileged background nor had many of his Progressive followers or, for that matter, Stegner himself. Their response to the sublime wilderness had been moderated by an equally strong sense of the limits it imposed on human aspirations. These Midwesterners had also brought to conservation and planning a nationalist outlook and fervor which over the years of the twentieth century had turned an elite reform enterprise into a broad-based democratic movement.

Stegner would also have been tempted to point out to the critics of traditional wilderness preservation the fact that Aldo Leopold's new "citizen" was neither an urban type wholly unfamiliar with rural life nor the beleaguered farmer or logger working for corporate interests. Instead, these environmental stewards were likely to be intellectuals who in their careers traversed the middle ground extending from downtown colleges and universities out through surrounding suburbs and into Sand County territory on the edge of a rougher and wilder world. These recruits to Aldo Leopold's doctrine of stewardship were intent on tending, repairing, and protecting all three segments of the American landscape. The Stegners themselves were active members of this intellectual vanguard, which not long ago Benny DeVoto had attempted to rally. Wallace and Mary watched over their Los Altos neighborhood and helped organize it against the incursion of developers promoting gated communities. They lavished the same care on the Greensboro place, tending, planting, and fixing. His Los Altos neighbors noticed the "easeful kind of order" Stegner imposed on his grounds. John Daniel, a young instructor who lived on the property for a while, described Wally's *modus operandi*: "He would move from task to task around the place, weeding here and fertilizing there, pruning the roses, rooting out a shot lemon tree and planting another, spading a new bed." There was one routine in particular that Stegner called "idiot's delight," collecting all the limbs and twigs and cutting them up for kindling. A suburban land ethic but also a life-long frugal habit.

As he grew older Stegner became increasingly active in regional and state preservation work, joining friends and colleagues intent on saving as much of the Plateau Province and the California coastline as possible. Throughout the eighties and early nineties he kept up his vigorous support of a range of national organizations as well. But his writing—the huge output of essays, articles, lectures, and reviews—formed the center of his attention, now directed toward two antienvironmental presidencies. Even as he grew more impassioned and impatient with Reagan and his successor he refused to stoop to name-calling and hatemongering. As another of his younger friends, Charles Wilkinson, observed, his principles required him to live in a civil way: "His ideas about the rigor of civility became so formidable because his thinking and writing were so rigorous." He put his strongest condemnations in the mouths of his fictional creations, as in the novel *A Shooting Star*, where his heroine describes her real estate developer brother as a man who "denuded and uglified the earth." "His kind never anticipated consequences. He was the kind that left eroded gulches and cut-over timberlands and man-made deserts and jerry-built tracts that would turn to slums in less than a generation."

As he turned eighty in 1989 Stegner's health continued to deteriorate and he was forced to cut back on the yard work he so enjoyed. The ball joint in one hip gave him a pronounced limp, constant discomfort, and the need for a cane. An anti-inflammatory drug tore up his stomach lining, and he gave up drinking except for an occasional glass of wine. In 1990 he suffered a severely sprained back, and the following year underwent a hip replacement operation. Even his hands and wrists gave him difficulty. He complained with as much good nature as he could muster. "I'm typing with one finger of one hand," he wrote Charles Wilkinson, "because walking with a cane has buggered my left wrist. Please forgive typos. The slower I go the more typos I make." Then a hopeful thought: "Maybe when the new hip is in place I'll even recover the use of my hands, and will stand before you transfigured, restored to my youthful vigor, ready for fun or frolic."

Recovery was not in the cards. In March 1993, he and Mary went to Santa Fe, where he was to receive yet another award. In a rented car Wallace pulled out of a side road to cross a main highway and was broadsided by an oncoming car. He suffered a collapsed lung, multiple broken ribs, and a broken collarbone, but was expected to survive. He was beginning to improve when he contracted pneumonia and then suffered a fatal heart attack. He died in the hospital on April 12, 1993.

In the years following his death there have appeared memorial volumes, personal recollections, and numerous critical appraisals of Stegner's life and work. In one of them, T.H. Watkins, a good friend in Wallace's later years, remembered that when Bernard DeVoto died in 1955 Stegner had said that the one big question his friends and colleagues asked was 'Who will do his work?' "In the midst of the hurt we feel at Stegner's death, the same sad insistent question lingers, though with a different inflection now: who will do *his* work?" All over the country were people like Michigan Congressman David Bonior who, on the enthusiastic recommendation of his staff, began reading Stegner without having heard of him and was so moved by his work that he went to hear him read. Listening to him, Bonior suddenly felt a close connection to Stegner, a man he'd never met. He went on to quote from Stegner on the nature of friendship. "Friendship is a relationship that has no formal shape, there are no rules or obligations or bonds as in marriage or the family. It is held together by neither law nor property nor blood, there is no glue in it but mutual liking." Here was a sufficient explanation of Stegner's own enduring friendship with Bernard DeVoto and of his lasting relationship with a national community of readers who, having read him, think they know him and know they like him.

Notes

Legacy

In addition to "Jonathan Dyer, Frontiersman," *Harper's* (September 1933), pp. 491–501, which DeVoto reprinted in *Forays and Rebuttals* (Boston: Little, Brown, 1936), he covered much of his childhood in "Fossil Remnants of the Frontier: Notes on a Utah Boyhood," *Harper's* (April 1935), pp. 590–600, and "A Sagebrush Bookshelf," *Harper's* (October 1937), pp. 488–496. The Wasatch country appears at a fictionalized distance in his first and last novels: *The Crooked Mile* (New York: Minton, Balch & Company, 1924) and *Mountain Time* (Boston: Little, Brown, 1947). DeVoto's first collection of essays, *Forays and Rebuttals*, included "The Plundered Province" (*Harper's*, 1934) along with his classic indictment of Mormonism, "The Centennial of Mormonism," and his celebration of New England, "New England: There She Stands." Patricia Limerick and Douglas Brinkley (eds.), *The West Against Itself*, a collection of DeVoto pieces, is forthcoming from Yale University Press. For a running account of DeVoto's career down to 1940 as elsewhere I have relied on Wallace Stegner's closely researched and engagingly written biography.

Stegner provides an account of his own early boyhood years in Eastend in *Wolf Willow: A History, a Story, and a Memoir of the Last Plains Frontier* (Lincoln: University of Nebraska Press, 1980, first published in New York: Viking, 1962) and in fictionalized form in *The Big Rock Candy Mountain* (Lincoln: University of Nebraska Press, 1983, first published in New York: Duell, Sloan & Pearce, 1943) for the early years and in *Recapitulation* (Garden City, N.Y.: Doubleday, 1979) for his adolescence and young manhood in Salt Lake City. He included a loving tribute to his mother, "Letter, Much Too Late," in *Where the Bluebird Sings to the Lemonade Springs* (New York: Random House, Penguin, 1992), pp. 22–33.

History

DeVoto collected his impressions of New York City in two "Easy Chair" pieces included in *Minority Report* (Boston: Little Brown, 1940): "On Moving to New York," *Harper's* (November 1936) and "On Moving from New York," *Harper's* (August 1938). His ongoing battles against both the literary left and the right are chronicled in the following "Easy Chair" and *Saturday Review* pieces, all of them collected in *Forays and Rebuttals* and *Minority Report*. "Thinking About America" (January 1934); "The Well-Informed, 1920–1930" (March 1931); "Exile's Return by Malcolm Cowley," *The Saturday Review* (June 2, 1934); "Proletarian Literature in the United States by Joseph Freeman," *The Saturday Review* (October 5, 1935). In editing his collection of DeVoto letters Stegner included in the section entitled "The Writing of History" the 1933 letter to Garrett Mattingly announcing his discovery of his culture hero (*The Letters of Bernard DeVoto* [Garden City, N.Y.: Doubleday, 1975], pp. 266–267). Stegner also included DeVoto's encouraging letter on his own draft of

Beyond the Hundredth Meridian in the same section. Stegner's developing centrist liberalism can be traced in both his factual and fictional works: *Fire and Ice* (New York: Duell, Sloan & Pearce, 1941); *Joe Hill: A Biographical Novel* (Lincoln: University of Nebraska Press, 1980, first published as *The Preacher and the Slave* [Boston: Houghton Mifflin, 1950]). The recently rediscovered *One Nation* (Boston: Houghton Mifflin, 1945) is a remarkably prescient analysis of race, minorities, and prejudice in the United States and an early call for cultural pluralism.

Land

DeVoto's story of the Rocky Mountain fur trade, *Across the Wide Missouri* (Boston: Houghton Mifflin, 1947) was followed by his history of the Spanish, French, and British frontiers down to the Lewis and Clark Expedition, *The Course of Empire* (Boston: Houghton Mifflin, 1952). DeVoto provided a running account of his war against the grazing interests in his last collection of "Easy Chair" pieces, *The Easy Chair* (Boston: Houghton Mifflin, 1955), grouped under the heading "Treatise on a Function of Journalism." In his *Letters of Bernard DeVoto* Stegner included a selection of DeVoto's letters on conservation and the public domain written to friends and foes alike.

Stegner's "Lake Powell" essay originally appeared in *Holiday* (May 1966), pp. 64–68, 148–151. In their *Wallace Stegner* (Boston: Twayne, 1977) Forrest and Margaret Robinson provide a full list of Stegner's uncollected articles down to 1975, pp. 178–182. Stegner's major fictional works in the years following his resignation from Stanford are: *Angle of Repose* (Garden City, N.Y.: Doubleday, 1971); *The Spectator Bird* (Garden City, N. Y.: Doubleday, 1976); *Recapitulation* (Garden City, N.Y.: Doubleday, 1979); *Crossing to Safety* (New York: Random House, 1987). *The Uneasy Chair* was published by Doubleday in 1974.

Jon Cosco, *Echo Park: Struggle for Preservation* (Boulder, Colo.: Johnson Books, 1995) is a lively and informed account of the battle to save Dinosaur National Monument from the dam builders and contains an introduction by David Brower.

Reprise

Stegner wrote four articles on Ansel Adams. His "Ansel Adams and the Search for Perfection" in *One Way to Spell Man* (Garden City, N.Y.: Doubleday, 1982) connects the artistry of his friend with the vision. William Cronon's Introduction and lead essay, "The Trouble with Wilderness; or, Getting Back to the Wrong Nature," in *Uncommon Ground: Toward Reinventing Nature* (New York: Norton, 1995), makes the case against purist advocates of wilderness preservation. Stegner's strongest indictment of Western land policy appeared in "The Spoiling of the American West," *Michigan Quarterly Review* (Spring 1987), pp. 293–310.

The critical assessments and appreciations of Stegner as man and writer which I have drawn on here are collected in Curt Meine, ed., *Wallace Stegner and the Continental Vision: Essays on Literature, History, and Landscape* (Washington, D.C., and Covelo, Calif.: Island Press, 1997). Particularly helpful are John Daniel, "Wallace Stegner's Hunger for Wholeness," T.H. Watkins, "Reluctant Tiger: Wallace Stegner Takes Up the Conservation Mantle," and Richard Knight, "Field Report from the New American West." Page Stegner and Mary Stegner edited a collection of tributes to Wallace by friends, colleagues, and students: *The Geography of Hope* (San Francisco: Sierra Club Books, 1996). Jackson J. Benson's *Wallace Stegner: A Study of the Short Fiction* (New York: Twayne, 1998) analyzes Stegner's shorter fiction and provides further analysis and commentary by several critics. James R. Hepworth, *Stealing Glances: Three Interviews with Wallace Stegner* (Albuquerque: University of New Mexico Press, 1998) contains retrospective views and opinions from the later years.

Sources

Both the DeVoto Papers and the Stegner Papers are housed in Stanford University's Green Library. Indispensable as introductions to DeVoto and Stegner are the two major biographies: Wallace Stegner, *The Uneasy Chair: A Biography of Bernard DeVoto* (Garden City, N.Y.: Doubleday, 1974); and Jackson J. Benson, *Wallace Stegner: His Life and Work* (New York: Viking, 1996). Both provide full accounts of their subjects' lives and times. Stegner's study of his friend is rich in detail and anecdote, and Benson's account is particularly helpful in interpreting Stegner's major works. Also useful are two briefer studies: Orlan Sawey, *Bernard DeVoto* (New York: Twayne, 1969), and Forrest G. Robinson and Margaret G. Robinson, *Wallace Stegner* (Boston: Twayne, 1977). *Four Portraits and One Subject: Bernard DeVoto* (Boston: Houghton Mifflin, 1963) contains four appreciative portraits of DeVoto by Catherine Drinker Bowen, Edith Mirrielees, Arthur Schlesinger, Jr., and Wallace Stegner together with a bibliography compiled by Julius P. Barclay in collaboration with Elaine Helmer Parnie. Benson's biography provides a full list of Stegner's novels, short story collections, histories, biographies, autobiographies, letters, and interviews. Richard Etulain, ed., *Conversations with Wallace Stegner about Western Literature and History* (Salt Lake City: University of Utah Press, 1983) collects Stegner's ideas and impressions of his own work as well as that of other Western writers.

Both DeVoto and Stegner periodically took account of their ideas in collections of their essays. DeVoto's selections are included in: *Forays and Rebuttals* (Boston: Little, Brown, 1936); *Minority Report* (Boston: Little, Brown, 1940); and *The Easy Chair* (Boston: Houghton Mifflin, 1955). Stegner's collections of essays are more numerous:

> *The Sound of Mountain Water* (Lincoln: University of Nebraska Press, 1985, first published in Garden City, N.Y.: Doubleday, 1969).
>
> *This Is Dinosaur: Echo Park Country and Its Magic Rivers* (Boulder, Colo.: Roberts Rinehard, 1985, first published in New York: Knopf, 1955).
>
> *One Way to Spell Man* (Garden City, N.Y.: Doubleday, 1982).
>
> *American Places*, with Page Stegner (Moscow: University of Idaho Press, 1983).
>
> *The American West as Living Space* (Ann Arbor: University of Michigan Press, 1987).
>
> *Where the Bluebird Sings to the Lemonade Springs* (New York: Random House, Penguin, 1992).

In order of publication DeVoto's histories are: *The Year of Decision: 1846* (Boston: Little, Brown, 1943); *Across the Wide Missouri* (Boston: Houghton Mifflin, 1947); and *The Course of Empire* (Boston: Houghton Mifflin, 1952). Stegner's histories are: *Mormon Country* (Lincoln: University of Nebraska Press, 1981, first published in New York: Duell, Sloan & Pearce, 1942); *The Gathering of Zion: The Story of the Mormon Trail* (Salt Lake City: Westwater Press,

1981, first published in New York: McGraw-Hill, 1964). In addition there are history essays in *Wolf Willow: A History, a Story, and a Memoir of the Last Plains Frontier* (Lincoln: University of Nebraska Press, 1980, first published in New York: Viking, 1962). A year after he published his biography of DeVoto, Stegner edited a selection of De Voto's letters which included the supportive and encouraging letters to Stegner as he struggled with his biography of John Wesley Powell, *The Letters of Bernard DeVoto* (Garden City, N.Y.: Doubleday, 1975).

There are several collections of appraisals of Stegner's work as well as recollections of the man himself. Among them is Anthony Arthur, ed., *Critical Essays on Wallace Stegner* (Boston: G.K. Hall, 1982) which contains Mary Ellen Williams Walsh's negative evaluation of *Angle of Repose*, "Angle of Repose and the Writings of Mary Hallock Foote: A Source Study." Also see Charles E. Rankin, ed., *Wallace Stegner: Man and Writer* (Albuquerque: University of New Mexico Press, 1996), and Curt Meine, ed., *Wallace Stegner and the Continental Vision: Essays on Literature, History, and Landscape* (Washington, D.C., and Covelo, Calif.: Island Press, 1997).

Index